Praise for *Yoga*

"I love *Yoga for the Brain*! It is a great way to relax, unwind and play. **Even better, research shows that games like these can have a mind-body benefit no matter how old you are. Sign me up for more!"**
—*Camille Leon, Founder, Holistic Chamber of Commerce.*

"Never before have I seen such a book, with word search puzzles, secret messages, and even more for the reader to enjoy! More than just a word search puzzle book, it's also packed with facts and information. Sitting down with the book is a great way to relax and stretch those brain muscles. I can see why the puzzles are considered 'yoga for the brain!' **This book is highly recommended for those looking for puzzles, relaxation, inspiration, and enjoyment!"**
—*Carla Trueheart for* Readers' Favorite

"*Yoga for the Brain* is inspirational, relevant, and fun! The puzzles are challenging in a good way, and the messages are insightful and meaningful. **It's well worth your time. I highly recommend it to everyone looking for something uniquely uplifting.** It provides an all-around positive experience anyone can benefit from. The books encompass food for thought and food for the soul!"
—*Brenda Krueger Huffman, Publisher,* Women's Voices Magazine

"Cristina Smith's **fun and easily accessible works brilliantly blend quantum consciousness-based science with profound philosophical wisdom.**"
—*Dr. Amit Goswami, Quantum Physicist and bestselling author of* The Self-Aware Universe

"While I've never actually heard the term 'yoga for the brain' before, it makes total sense. This book easily fulfills the mental and spiritual aspects of a Yoga practice. **So much more than a puzzle book, the fun facts, history, and education lining the pages make Yoga for the Brain books a unique treasure.** I highly recommend it for an entertaining and enlightening experience!"

—*Sheri Hoyte for* Reader Views

"Everything Cristina writes about in her books is about our choice of what to do with the great gift of life we have been given. She has experienced in her own life the power of the spirit to transform her life and allow her to tap into her energy and enthusiasm to help others become all they can be. Puzzles are half of what these books are about. The other half is the commentary Cristina provides that helps us to learn to live fully in this present moment. Highly recommended!"

—*Dr. Russell Fanelli, Professor Emeritus, Western New England University*

Highly Recommended!
    —*The Wishing Shelf, UK*

The *Yoga for the Brain*™ series has earned more than a dozen literary awards in the United States and United Kingdom. Have fun discovering why by looking inside!

Animal Wisdom Word Search
Yoga for the Brain™

Cristina Smith
Rick Smith
Lauren McCall

A POST HILL PRESS BOOK
ISBN: 978-1-64293-130-3

Animal Wisdom Word Search:
Yoga for the Brain™
© 2019 by Cristina Smith and Rick Smith
All Rights Reserved

Post Hill Press
New York • Nashville
posthillpress.com

Published in the United States of America

Table of Contents

Foreword 1

How Do We Talk to the Animals? 2

How to Play 6

How to Find the Words 7

Colorful Tip 9

About the Animal Messages 9

The Power of Animal Wisdom 30

Can We *Really* Talk to the Animals? 52

The Puzzle of Intelligence 74

Going Beyond the Beyond 98

Time for the Yoga of Now 122

End Game 146

Answers 149

Gratitude and Appreciation 161

Biographies 163

Foreword

Dear Lauren,

You've been part of our lives for a long time. You are kind and loving to every animal, and to a lot of us, too. You've reminded us of love, and how important it is to express love in everything we do. Here's our thanks and joy for the gifts you've given to us and to all the world—in your books, and your meetings, and the talks you've shared with so many of us.

We know that there are others who need the gift of your presence and your wisdom. You're probably learning, too, and meeting different animals, talking with them, telling them that, in spite of the cruelties they may have lived, that most humans love them and would rescue them all, if we could.

Thank you for touching our lives, and joy for the brilliant life you've led! Thank you for being with us and showing the way for us to live gently together. And of course, thanks to you, we've already improved in this lifetime, as we continue living and loving all life.

—*Richard Bach*
Author of Jonathan Livingston Seagull

How Do We Talk to the Animals?

Do you talk to your pets? Many of us do. Whether letting them know when we will be back home or that we love them, animals often share the daily moments of our lives. First recorded in the 14th century, the word *animal* comes from the Latin *animalis,* which means "having breath or soul."

Oddly enough, it seems that somewhere over the centuries, we humans have excluded ourselves from the animal kingdom. Some see humans as superior. Many quote biblical references about dominion. But what does that really mean? Depends on who you ask. Does dominion imply a sense of responsibility? What if it meant we were to care for, protect, and preserve the other critters we share our planet with?

Though we have different kinds of intelligences and bodies than other animals, it has taken all species coexisting and evolving to make our world into the natural wonder it is today. Researchers demonstrate again and again that many creatures, including the dolphin, elephant, octopus, and our 97-percent-DNA-match ape brethren, exhibit consciousness and self-awareness.

Do you ever wonder what your animal companion is trying to say to you? According to our guest artist and animal communicator Lauren McCall, we *can* hear their voices. In this book, you will hear their voices too.

Interspecies communication happens every day. Interactions with our animal family members reflect a form of spoken, yet not necessarily verbal dialogue. We learn to discern the subtlety of various meows. Cat lovers are particularly taken with the silent meow, which seems to reach straight to the heart. Dog barks have different tones and meaning, from *Let's play!* to *I'm hungry!* to *Get out of my yard!* We share a private, deeply personal language with the other species in our lives.

Communication is not a one-way street, nor is there just one way to communicate. Animals interact with each other using signals that are visual, auditory, chemical, and electrical. They also communicate beyond physical language; we would almost call it vibrational, or even telepathy.

Telepathy is information transmitted from one individual to another without means of the five senses. We send out a signal which could be an intention, feeling, thought, or image. That signal can be received by someone tuning into our channel. Likewise, we can receive transmissions from others when we dial in to their unique frequency.

Sometimes called extra sensory perception or clairvoyance, telepathy is really not so mysterious. It is something that we all know how to do. After all, it's how we communicated as newborn babies. How many moms have you seen enter the room before the first cry? We just need to re-discover the skill and practice it, if we are so inclined.

Lauren has spent decades training and honing her intuitive and telepathic skills as an interspecies communicator. The animal wisdom message puzzles are transcriptions of her conversations with a wide variety of species. Lauren teaches around the world and encourages students to go deeply into their hearts to tune in to this process of receiving information.

> I think what is being transmitted during a telepathic communication is the essence behind the words. It is the feeling or intent that is being sent to me, rather than the actual word itself. My "satellite dish" picks up the intent of what the animals are saying and translates it into a format I can understand. The satellite dish for my TV at home works the same way.

—Lauren McCall

Our planet is filled with extraordinary, conscious creatures that are living their own lives, flourishing in their own right. Animals have many gifts to offer us, if only we have the heart, mind, and soul to receive their wisdom and love. Listen with your heart the next time your animal companion says *Meow! Woof!* or *Tweet!* The message you receive might be a surprise, or it may be a message of love that your heart already knows.

Let's Play!

Have Fun!

How to Play

A word search puzzle consists of letters placed in a grid. Some of the letters form words, others not. The object of this game is to find and mark all the words hidden inside the grid that appear in the accompanying word list. The words may be placed horizontally, vertically, or diagonally, and arranged forward or backward, depending on the difficulty level of the puzzle.

There are two levels of puzzles. The first 10 puzzles will get you started. The words you are looking for in the grid are spelled forward. They can be found in a horizontal, vertical, or diagonal line and may share letters with other words.

Puzzles 11–60 are advanced. There are more words hidden in the grid and they might be backward as well as forward.

Hidden within the puzzle is a secret message created by the letters that are not used in any word within the grid. The key to decoding it is underneath the text of the reading. The blank lines are where you will place the letters discovered once the word search phase of the puzzle is complete. Starting from the top left corner of the puzzle grid and proceeding left to right, line by line, place each unused letter in the blank in the order it occurs. When solved, an Animal Wisdom message associated with the reading magically appears!

How to Find the Words

Knowing where to start is sometimes
the key to the solution.

There is no one right way to solve these word search puzzles. It's individual. Your unique brilliance will reveal your perfect way forward. Word search puzzles are a wonderful way to play with your brain and help increase its flexibility. Experiment with these different strategies and notice how it feels when doing each. It is likely that one approach will feel more natural.

What's great about playing with your brain in this context is that it is a no-risk proposition. Nothing critical is on the line. There is no deadline. No one else will be judging your performance. It is the perfect laboratory in which to do research on yourself. A whole brain approach could look something like this:

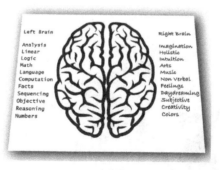

Start with the right brain intuitive approach. Read the conversation. Scan the grid and see what words you notice first. Circle them and cross them off the list. It is interesting to make a note of the ones that pop out at as an indicator of your current state of being.

Take a look at the word list and then look again at the grid and see what else reveals itself. Consider picking out a word and see if you are able to find it by shifting your perspective.

Next, move to the left brain logical strategy. A common tactic for finding all the words is to go through the puzzle left to right (or vice versa) and look for the first letter of the word. After finding the letter, look at the eight surrounding letters to see whether the next letter of the word is there. Continue this system until the entire word is found.

The step-by-step method approaches the word list in order. It's helpful to skip over the ones that are elusive at the moment and come back to those words later.

To finish, switch on the right brain intuitive technique again. Which words did you have a hard time finding? Notice anything interesting about them? Isn't it fascinating what we see and don't see?

Get to know yourself in different states of mind.
New perspectives emerge.

  Cristina Smith and Rick Smith with Lauren McCall

Colorful Tip

Many people use a pencil to circle found words and then cross or check them off the list. That works well, especially if you have a good eraser. However, the grid looks a bit chaotic when all of the word list is found. As a colorful tip, use a highlighter felt tip pen to identify found words in the grid. It can make it easier to recognize which letters remain unused when decoding the secret message.

About the Animal Messages

Each puzzle includes a conversation that guest artist Lauren McCall has actually had with the animal. In some instances, she is asking questions and speaking on behalf of a human family member.

Aslan the Cat

Aslan is a very cool orange cat with some strong opinions about who animals are. Like most cats, he sleeps an average of sixteen to eighteen hours per day. Happy both indoors and outside, he is a fearless hunter who survived a rattlesnake bite.

Lauren: What do you want people to know about animals?

Aslan: We have paths that are our own, not just a part of yours. People can be very egotistical when they see animals only as related to themselves. Humans must look outside themselves and realize that the planet is crisscrossed by millions, billions of paths. The human path may be broader, and often more destructive, but each being, any being, is on their path. I think there are some animals wiser than some people.

Lauren: Yes, that has been my experience too.

Aslan: Anyway, I am not so mighty, or special. But I am unique, as are you. Living together, you have let me be my best, and my worst. You have let me learn. In doing that, you have also learned. This is worth reflecting on. I am moving on my path in my own Aslan way.

Lauren: What does that mean?

Aslan: Cute, charming, stylish, and a bit wild. I am a warrior of life!

Animal Wisdom:

___ ___ ___   ___ ___ ___ ___ ___ ___   ___ ___ ___ ___
___ ___ ___ ___ ___ ___ ___ ___ ___ ___   ___ ___ ___ ___
___ ___ ___ ___ ___ ___ ___   ___ ___ ___ ___ ___ ___ ___   ___ ___ ___
___ ___ ___   ___ ___   ___ ___ ___ ___ ___   ___ ___   ___ ___ ___ ___ ___

```
A L W O R A N G E L B B E I
N G O S H A V C U T E E I M
N B R O A D E R D I S V I I
D U S U R E F L E C T I N G
A N T T O G E T H E R L P H
W I L D A O P I N I O N S T
T Q F P A T H H S H A P P Y
W U E A N I M A L S E A V L
I E A W S S P E C I A L N E
G T R A T T L E S N A K E A
O G L R Y I E T H W I S E R
E R E R L C H A R M I N G N
T H S I I A S L A N E W E B
O F S O S L E E P S L I F E
O N E R H U N T E R A R T H
```

Animals	Hunter	Special
Aslan	Learn	Stylish
Best	Mighty	Together
Broader	Opinions	Unique
Charming	Orange	Warrior
Cute	Path	Wild
Egotistical	Rattlesnake	Wiser
Fearless	Reflecting	Worst
Happy	Sleeps	

Allie the Dog

Allie, a delightful mixed terrier, is adopted. Of the 3.3 million dogs who enter shelters in the U.S. each year, only about half find forever homes.

Lauren: What makes you happy?

Allie: Waking up every morning. Every day has such great possibilities.

Lauren: I'm glad you feel that way.

Allie: Well, look at my life now compared with where I came from. I was content enough before. You may as well be happy with what you have, right? But now I have my family, my dog friends to play with, my own yard with trees, and there are walnuts on the ground to eat. Also, there are squirrels to chase. All of that makes me happy.

Lauren: Especially the squirrels I think?

Allie: They keep me sharp and I have to run my fastest to catch them. Though, I have never actually caught one. It's more about the fun of the chase; it's a game.

Lauren: Do the squirrels understand that it's a game?

Allie: Oh sure. They taunt me to chase them. They know they can always run up a tree. It's playing the game and having fun that counts.

Lauren: So it's not about catching the squirrel?

Allie: No. That would be mean. Besides, then the game would be over and where is the fun in that? It's more fun to play.

Animal Wisdom:

____ __ _____ ____
_____ ___
_____ _____ __ ___

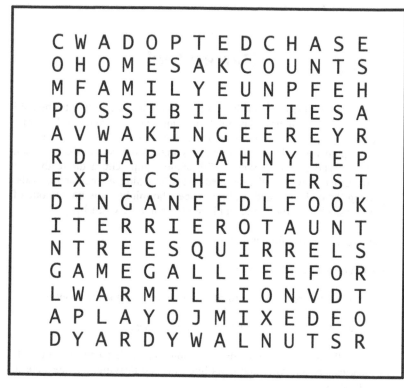

```
C W A D O P T E D C H A S E
O H O M E S A K C O U N T S
M F A M I L Y E U N P F E H
P O S S I B I L I T I E S A
A V W A K I N G E E R E Y R
R D H A P P Y A H N Y L E P
E X P E C S H E L T E R S T
D I N G A N F F D L F O O K
I T E R R I E R O T A U N T
N T R E E S Q U I R R E L S
G A M E G A L L I E E F O R
L W A R M I L L I O N V D T
A P L A Y O J M I X E D E O
D Y A R D Y W A L N U T S R
```

Adopted	Friends	Shelters
Allie	Game	Squirrels
Chase	Glad	Taunt
Compared	Happy	Terrier
Content	Homes	Trees
Counts	Million	Waking
Delightful	Mixed	Walnuts
Family	Play	Yard
Feel	Possibilities	
Forever	Sharp	

Barred Owl

Every year in Quebec, Canada, groups of volunteers go out into the cold April night to count the owl populations. One year I joined them. To attract the birds, we project recordings of owl calls out into the forests. The barred owl is quite vocal. The sounds that they make often sound like a human saying, "Who cooks for you?" With audio equipment at the ready, our group drove down small tree-lined roads, stopping at regular intervals, playing the owl calls, and waiting to see who might show up. On one of our stops, a barred owl came and landed in a tree very nearby.

Lauren: Thank you for coming.

Owl: You are not what I expected.

Lauren: You were expecting to find another owl. I'm sorry about that.

Owl: What do you want? What are you doing here?

Lauren: We are here to count the owl population in this area so that people can ensure that you, and owls like you, are thriving. We are here to count owls.

Owl: How silly. There are as many as there are!

Animal Wisdom:

__ __ __ __ __ __   __ __ __ __   __ __ __
__ __ __ __ __ __ __   __ __   __ __ __ __   __ __ __
__ __ __ __ __ __ __   __ __   __ __ __ __ __ __

```
S P R O J E C T R E A D Y T
I H I E C E B A R R E D N G
L E S T C A Q H T H R I V E
L A X T V O L U N T E E R S
Y A R P E O R L I V R B V I
Q U E B E C I D S P O A O U
C S H O W C N S I T M C C O
P O P U L A T I O N S E A T
O U O W L P E E A M G E N L
A N R K E R R U D U N S A T
C D L E S I V L A N D E D A
R S T O P L A Y I N G I A O
B I R D S T L N I G H T O H
E R F O R E S T C O U N T S
```

April	Expected	Ready
Attract	Forest	Recordings
Audio	Intervals	Show
Barred	Landed	Silly
Birds	Night	Sounds
Calls	Owl	Thrive
Canada	Playing	Vocal
Cooks	Population	Volunteers
Count	Project	
Equipment	Quebec	

Saddle-Billed Stork

The saddle-billed stork is the largest of the African storks and can weigh up to twenty pounds. Standing between five and six feet tall, their wing span can be up to nine feet. Since they have no muscles in their voice box, they are silent. Saddle-billed storks rattle their bills to make noise and communicate. When we met, this industrious female was wading in the water looking for food. She was very focused on her task. I felt that I was a bit of a distraction.

Lauren: You look like you are searching for something.

Stork: Looking, looking, looking for food. Little fish, little fish.

Lauren: I hope you find some. You are very pretty.

Stork: Yes, pretty. And often looking, looking.

Lauren: Do you often find fish?

Stork: Oh yes. Many, many fish. Big fish, little fish. All sorts of fish, fish. Little frogs too.

Lauren: Yes, I have seen many small frogs myself. They are very pretty too.

Stork: Pretty frogs are delicious!

Lauren: Do you have time to notice the beauty around you?

Stork: Yes, there is much beauty. Open land, and lots of water. Pretty fish, frogs, bugs, and birds. The water is so beautiful, and the sounds, that it makes make me very happy. Water sounds like life to me!

Animal Wisdom:

__ __ __ __ __ __ __ __ __ __ __ __ __ __ __

__ __ __ __ __ __ __ __ __ __ __ __ __

__ __ __ __ __ __ __ __ __ __ __ __ __ __

__ __ __ __ __ __ __ __ __ __

```
W N O I S E A L V O I C E K
F I S H B E A U T Y S I N B
E O P E N A F R O G S P R U
T Y I A A P R E T T Y N A D
W I N G E R I W E I G H T N
N J D E L I C I O U S S T O
Y L U I B F A H E T H I L E
N E S V I E N L I T T L E R
Y T T B L O O K I N G E H I
N G R I L W A D I N G N W I
L L I R E N O U R W A T E R
F O O D D B U G S T O R K I
S M U S C L E S A D D L E H
D I S T R A C T I O N Y O U
```

African	Industrious	Silent
Beauty	Little	Span
Billed	Looking	Stork
Birds	Muscles	Voice
Bugs	Noise	Wading
Delicious	Open	Water
Distraction	Pretty	Weigh
Fish	Rattle	Wing
Food	Saddle	
Frogs	Searching	

Indie the Cat

A cat's nose is ridged with a unique pattern, just like a human fingerprint. They greet one another by touching their noses together or bumping heads, just as humans greet each other by shaking hands. A group of kittens is known as a *kindle*; adult cats are called a *clowder*. Indie is a cat with a big personality and a fun and helpful perspective on things.

Lauren: I want you to know that I love you very much.

Indie: Me too. I feel really happy when we are together. We are buddies, friends.

Lauren: Yes, we certainly are. When I go out to work, do you like it when I leave the radio on?

Indie: Yes, but I like it better when you are home.

Lauren: Me too. Unfortunately, I do have to work. It's one of those tedious human things that I have to do.

Indie: Yes, humans have a lot of odd things they do.

Lauren: Like what?

Indie: Laundry. You have to take your clothes off to wash. I don't. I wash and wear my fur!

Lauren: Your system is more efficient. Warmer too.

Indie: Also we come in pretty colors.

Lauren: Humans do too.

Indie: Really? Are they black like me?

Lauren: Sometimes. And many other lovely colors too.

Animal Wisdom:

— — — — — — — — — — — — —
— — — — — — — — — —
— — — — — — — — — — — — — — — — — —
— — — — — — — —

```
C F I N G E R P R I N T T H
E O P E R S P E C T I V E R
I C L O W D E R L O V E L Y
C C L O T H E S W E A R U H
N W E B R S T O U C H I N G
W A S H U S S N O G F D I C
F R I E N D S A O N R G Q N
E M C K I N D L E T S E U I
O E N B U M P I N G Y D E T
R R A N K I T T E N S S C T
E L A U N D R Y N S T D S C
I N D I E B L A C K E O L O
R P A T T E R N A N M D C L
O T N O S E H A P P Y H E S
```

Black	Happy	Perspective
Buddies	Indie	Ridged
Bumping	Kindle	System
Clothes	Kittens	Touching
Clowder	Laundry	Unique
Colors	Lovely	Warmer
Fingerprint	Nose	Wash
Friends	Pattern	Wear
Greet	Personality	

6 Lilac-Breasted Roller Bird

Birds have a different sort of genius than humans. From learning complex birdsongs to species-specific technical, social, spatial, inventive, artistic, and adaptive skills, being a *bird brain* may actually be quite a compliment. There are some 10,400 avian species living on our amazing planet. That means there are thirty times more wild birds than humans.

One of the most beautiful and colorful birds in sub-Saharan Africa is the lilac-breasted roller. Sitting on a low tree branch, one of these highly territorial, monogamous birds watched us as we walked by. The sun gently illuminated her colorful feathers, and I found her breathtaking.

Lauren: You are so beautiful.

Roller: I am beautiful. I am one of the most beautiful birds here.

Lauren: That is something to be proud of.

Roller: We are very proud birds. We are happy birds. Our colors reflect who we are—beautiful outside and beautiful inside.

Lauren: That's wonderful. Do you mind that we are passing through your area? We are trying not to disturb you.

Roller: You are most welcome guests. Especially if you admire me!

Animal Wisdom:

__ __ __ __ __ __ __ __ __ __ __ __ __ __

__ __ __ __ __ __ __ __ __ __ __ __

__ __ __ __ __ __ __ __ __ __ __

```
B P R O U D R O L L E R B E
R I I L L U M I N A T E D N
A L I L A C O L O R F U L G
I W I N V E N T I V E H O Y
N O F U A C O M P L E X R G
G U E S T S G W E L C O M E
S E A B B E A U T I F U L N
O S T R C R M D A V I A N I
C K H E T E O B A D A T E U
I I E A S I U B R P M E A S
A L R S U T S S P A T I A L
L L S T Y I N T S I N I R D
E S P E C I E S I A N C V E
D O U D R E F L E C T T H E
```

Adaptive	Complex	Reflect
Admire	Feathers	Roller
Artistic	Genius	Skills
Avian	Guests	Social
Beautiful	Illuminated	Spatial
Brain	Inventive	Species
Branch	Lilac	Welcome
Breasted	Monogamous	
Colorful	Proud	

Giraffe

The planet's tallest mammal, the giraffe is able to clean its ears with its own tongue. Their spot patterns are unique to each individual. I spoke with this wise zoo giraffe.

Lauren: What do you like about being a giraffe?

Giraffe: Looking down on everything gives you a very different perspective I think. I am physically removed from what goes on below, and can feel emotionally detached too.

Lauren: Is that an advantage?

Giraffe: It is when you live in a zoo. This is a very strange, artificial environment. No matter how the keepers try, it is make-believe. We are not in the land of our ancestors.

Lauren: And how does your very tall perspective help you?

Giraffe: I feel emotionally removed, distant. I am here, but do not feel a part of this place.

Lauren: Are you avoiding your reality?

Giraffe: I am creating my own reality. How I see and feel things is my reality. I just choose not to participate in this illusion that the zoo has created to be my reality.

Lauren: How very interesting.

Giraffe: Reality is what you make it, and how you perceive it. In places like this, you can either fully embrace the enclosure where you live, or you can filter yourself and spend only as much energy as is necessary in the physical environment. Being a giraffe, I'm always reminded to *rise above it all*.

Animal Wisdom:

__ __ __ __ __ __ __ __ __

__ __ __ __ __ __ __ __ __ __ __ __

__ __ __ __ __ __ __ __ __ __ __ __ __

__ __ __ __ __ __ __

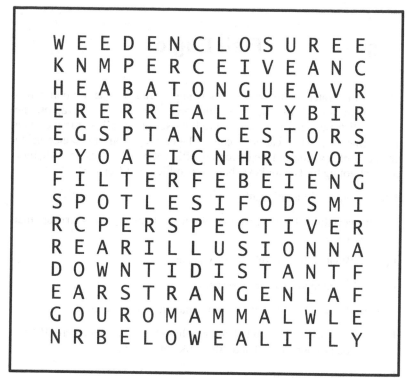

```
W E E D E N C L O S U R E E
K N M P E R C E I V E A N C
H E A B A T O N G U E A V R
E R E R R E A L I T Y B I R
E G S P T A N C E S T O R S
P Y O A E I C N H R S V O I
F I L T E R F E B E I E N G
S P O T L E S I F O D S M I
R C P E R S P E C T I V E R
R E A R I L L U S I O N N A
D O W N T I D I S T A N T F
E A R S T R A N G E N L A F
G O U R O M A M M A L W L E
N R B E L O W E A L I T L Y
```

Above	Enclosure	Perceive
Ancestors	Energy	Perspective
Artificial	Environment	Reality
Below	Filter	Rise
Detached	Giraffe	Spot
Distant	Illusion	Strange
Down	Keepers	Tall
Ears	Mammal	Tongue
Embrace	Patterns	

Fish Eagle

Out on the water in Botswana's Okavango Delta, we came upon a fish eagle who was clearly surveying the area. Classified as a raptor, the African fish eagle has five times more light-sensitive cells in his eyes than the human eye. They can spot camouflaged prey from a distance using their complex vision and are extremely efficient hunters. Besides fish, they also eat young birds, monkeys, baby crocodiles, and frogs.

Lauren: What you looking at?

Eagle: Everything. I see everything. Not much happens in my territory that I don't see.

Lauren: What is the role of your species here?

Eagle: We are reporters and observers.

Lauren: What do you do with the information that you gather?

Eagle: Those who watch and observe help to keep a balance here. If I see too much of one thing, I and others like me will eat it.

Lauren: Fish, you mean?

Eagle: Yes. And what happens around here in my area is duplicated elsewhere. Balance must be kept.

Lauren: And do you think that people interfere with the balance of nature here?

Eagle: I don't think about people—they have nothing to do with my life. All are welcome here, if they come in peace.

Animal Wisdom:

— —————' — ———— ————

————— —————————————— ——

—————— ———— ——————————

————————

```
A C A M O U F L A G E D B I
R C R O B S E R V E A G L E
P P L O D T E R R I T O R Y
E R I E C H U N T E R S S C
A E G E A O D I S T A N C E
C Y H B I R D S Y I P E V L
E I T D U P L I C A T E D L
E W G I V B E Y L F O I S S
I N F R E P O R T E R S V O
R M A T D E L T A I S O O E
N T M O N K E Y S O C R G E
A T E F A N D M A W E Y E S
V I S I O N O K A V A N G O
I N T S A I N B A L A N C E
B A L H A W A T C H N C A E
```

Balance	Duplicated	Okavango
Birds	Eagle	Peace
Botswana	Eyes	Prey
Camouflaged	Fish	Raptor
Cells	Frogs	Reporters
Clearly	Hunters	Sensitive
Crocodiles	Light	Territory
Delta	Monkeys	Vision
Distance	Observe	Watch

Cape Buffalo

This fellow is an older, solitary, buffalo hanging around our cabin in Africa. He's known as a *dagga boy*—an older bull past his prime who has separated from his herd. He has four times the strength of an ox and an exceptional memory.

Lauren: How do you feel about our being here?

Buffalo: You are intruders, but respectful ones. I do not fear you.

Lauren: I'm glad because there is nothing to fear from the people in this camp. They want to live in peace and harmony.

Buffalo: That's really what we all want.

Lauren: Do you have friends of your species? Of any species?

Buffalo: We buffalo can talk to each other, but not friends exactly. I talk to the birds. Some of them keep me clean, some keep watch for me from above.

Lauren: What do they watch for?

Buffalo: Lion.

Lauren: Do you feel a sense of interconnectedness here?

Buffalo: Very much so. There is a rhythm that changes with the water and the weather. Water is king here, not animals, not humans. Water. Without it we all die, or move on. This area, this year, it is good. Plenty for everyone and there is real harmony.

Animal Wisdom:

___ ___ ___   ___ ___ ___ ___ ___ ___   ___ ___ ___   ___ ___ ___ ___ ___
___ ___ ___   ___ ___ ___ ___ ___ ___ ___   ___ ___   ___ ___ ___ ___ ___ ___
___ ___   ___ ___ ___   ___ ___ ___ ___ ___ ___

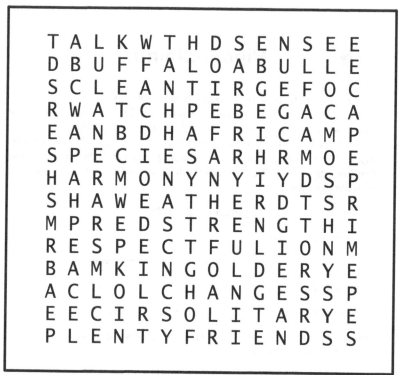

```
T A L K W T H D S E N S E E
D B U F F A L O A B U L L E
S C L E A N T I R G E F O C
R W A T C H P E B E G A C A
E A N B D H A F R I C A M P
S P E C I E S A R H R M O E
H A R M O N Y N Y I Y D S P
S H A W E A T H E R D T S R
M P R E D S T R E N G T H I
R E S P E C T F U L I O N M
B A M K I N G O L D E R Y E
A C L O L C H A N G E S S P
E E C I R S O L I T A R Y E
P L E N T Y F R I E N D S S
```

Africa	Harmony	Rhythm
Birds	Herd	Sense
Buffalo	Intruders	Solitary
Bull	King	Species
Cabin	Lion	Strength
Camp	Memory	Talk
Cape	Older	Watch
Changes	Peace	Water
Clean	Plenty	Weather
Dagga	Prime	
Friends	Respectful	

Hippopotamus

To stay cool in the blistering African heat, hippos spend most of their day in rivers and lakes. Their eyes, nose, and ears are located on the top of their heads, which means they can see and breathe while submerged in the water. They can hold their breath for up to five minutes. Hippos sweat an oily red liquid. It acts as sunblock and helps protect their thick yet sensitive skin from drying out. We came across this hippo while out on a small boat in Okavango Delta.

Lauren: We are watching you, do you mind?

Hippo: It is an intrusion.

Lauren: I know, I'm sorry. We have come to admire you.

Hippo: Oh, that's different.

Lauren: Why are you in this particular pool of water?

Hippo: It is a territorial issue. There is plenty of water and we are comfortable and well hidden.

Lauren: It's wonderful that you live on land and in the water.

Hippo: Yes, we are very versatile and we can move freely. We have a unique perspective above and below.

Lauren: Which do you prefer?

Hippo: We feel safest below the water, but there is more to see and it is more colorful above the water. Both have their positive points. There is a time for both.

Animal Wisdom:

— — — —   — —   —   — — — — — — — —
— — — — — — —   — — —   — — — — —   — —
— —   — — — —   — — —   — — —
— — — — — —   — —   — — —   — — — — — — —

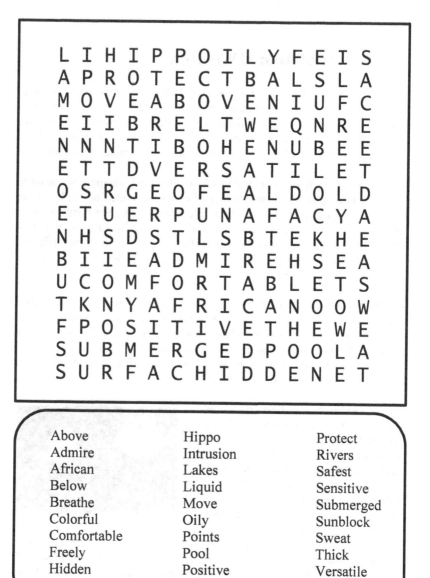

```
L I H I P P O I L Y F E I S
A P R O T E C T B A L S L A
M O V E A B O V E N I U F C
E I I B R E L T W E Q N R E
N N N T I B O H E N U B E E
E T T D V E R S A T I L E T
O S R G E O F E A L D O L D
E T U E R P U N A F A C Y A
N H S D S T L S B T E K H E
B I I E A D M I R E H S E A
U C O M F O R T A B L E T S
T K N Y A F R I C A N O O W
F P O S I T I V E T H E W E
S U B M E R G E D P O O L A
S U R F A C H I D D E N E T
```

Above	Hippo	Protect
Admire	Intrusion	Rivers
African	Lakes	Safest
Below	Liquid	Sensitive
Breathe	Move	Submerged
Colorful	Oily	Sunblock
Comfortable	Points	Sweat
Freely	Pool	Thick
Hidden	Positive	Versatile

The Power of Animal Wisdom

Are you quick as a bunny? Strong as an ox? Clever as a mongoose? Playful as a kitten? Much of human behavior is described in terms of our fellow animals' characteristics. Sometimes we call upon the talents and qualities associated with a particular animal. Many of these invocations have become common similes, phrases that compare one thing to another.

When up early in the morning while others are sleeping, we want to be quiet as a mouse. In situations that take more courage than we know we have, we want to be brave as a lion. We want to have the memory of an elephant. When we feel the need for transformation in our lives, we think of the incredible journey of the caterpillar, from cocoon to butterfly. Or from ugly duckling to graceful swan. We want to be loyal as a dog, wise as an owl, and eagle-eyed.

Sometimes we can be blind as a bat, stubborn as a mule, wily as a coyote, hungry as a horse, eager as a beaver, mysterious as a raven, joyful as a hummingbird, or strutting like a rooster. Smart as a fox, proud as a peacock, fat as a pig, a crashing boar, a bull in a china shop, busy as a bee, crazy as a loon, mad as a hornet, gentle as a lamb, fierce as a tiger, naked as a jaybird. We are all these things, and more.

In addition to these common sayings, there are inherent qualities of our fellow earthlings that we can cultivate to improve our well-being and personal evolution. Sometimes it's a good idea to take some time for hibernation and introspection, like the bear. Or enjoy some sunshine like a lizard on a rock. Or shed our skin like a snake. Out with the old, and in with the new, so we can grow into the next phase of life. When we call upon the symbolic power of an animal, we are asking to be drawn into complete harmony with the strength of that creature's essence. They may appear in dreams, meditation, or fly across the sky in our inner vision. Sometimes they even cross our paths while out for a walk in the moonlight.

  Cristina Smith and Rick Smith with Lauren McCall

Beyond the symbolic, there is deep wisdom in having animal companions. Just fifteen minutes spent bonding with an animal sets off a chemical chain reaction in the brain, lowering levels of the fight-or-flight hormone cortisol and increasing production of the feel-good hormone serotonin. The result? Heart rate, blood pressure, and stress levels immediately drop.*

Swimming with whale sharks and other sea creatures helps wounded warriors heal at the Georgia Aquarium in Atlanta. There are horse therapy centers nationwide and therapeutic riding centers for mentally, physically, and emotionally handicapped children of all ages. Some senior living facilities now have community animals like dogs and chickens onsite and many include pet caretaking as part of the residents' service plan. Over the long term, interspecies interactions can lower cholesterol levels, fight depression, and may even help protect against heart disease and stroke. Animals are just good medicine for humans.

Many people tend to like their animal compatriots better than other people. Our companion creatures are reliable, non-judgmental, and have no hidden motives. They listen politely and don't need money. They take us as we are and don't want or expect us to change. They are glad to see us when we come home. Animals help keep us from going too far down into deep pits of despair. No matter how we feel on the inside, they need to be fed and cared for. And when we care for and feed them, it reminds us to take care of ourselves. Besides all that, and most importantly, they love us unconditionally. And we love them right back.

* *Centers for Disease Control and Prevention*

Baby Elephant

There are more than forty thousand muscles in an elephant's trunk. A fusion of the upper lip and nose, it is sensitive enough to pick up objects as small as a penny and strong enough to lift whole trees.

The planet's largest mammal, baby elephants weigh around 200 pounds when born, after spending almost two years in the womb. When visiting a local zoo, I spotted this baby elephant when he was giving himself a dirt bath on a hot day. He really seemed to be enjoying himself and I found him irresistible.

Lauren: You seem to be enjoying your dirt bath.

Elephant: I am! I have as much dirt here as I want. It keeps me cool while it's so hot.

Lauren: Do you have a happy life?

Elephant: I enjoy being young and I feel free to learn and make mistakes. In my mind, I am free. Some of the older elephants, I think, would not agree with me. But for right now, I am happy and free, and I enjoy the dirt.

Lauren: I think it's wonderful that you are having such fun.

Elephant: The dirt is here for me to play with, and so I play with the dirt. Life is simple.

Animal Wisdom:

— — — — — — — — — — — — — — — — — —
— — — — — — — — — — — — — — — — — — — —
— — — — — — — — — — — — — — — — —

Cristina Smith and Rick Smith with Lauren McCall

```
H A Y A L P L E A R N P E P
I I N B E L E S N S A L N H
D R B T A R J O B J E C T S
L O R M T B E Y C P O A O S
H I M E O M S P H E B Y F T
D A F R S W E A P O L D E R
M O P E M I N T R U N K P O
U I T P H T S I M P L E N N
S E S F Y E I T S I N R O G
C E R T G M T P I N O I L E
L E S R A P I L Y B S E A S
E U A O R K V E S U L O O C
S L W O N D E R F U L E I N
L I P O U N D S M A L L F E
```

Baby	Largest	Pounds
Bath	Learn	Sensitive
Born	Life	Simple
Cool	Mammal	Small
Dirt	Mistakes	Strong
Elephant	Muscles	Tree
Enjoy	Nose	Trunk
Free	Objects	Upper
Fusion	Older	Womb
Happy	Penny	Wonderful
Irresistible	Play	

Malachite Kingfisher

These small, beautiful birds with bright, metallic-blue upper bodies live in sub-Saharan Africa. They live in bogs, swamps, marshes, estuaries, mangrove forests, and near rivers and streams. Kingfishers are the biggest birds that are able to hover in the air. They do not sing; instead they make a dry, loud screeching noise. Mates perform a duet, a series of calls ending with a chuckle. This particularly charming being lives in the Okavango Delta in Botswana.

Lauren: You are beautiful.

Kingfisher: I know. I am the jewel of the Delta. My colors capture the heart of the Delta. Yellow for the sun, blue for the sky, red for the plants below the water, green for the reeds and the leaves, and orange for the morning before the sun reaches high in the sky. I am everything in one bird.

Lauren: That is wonderful.

Kingfisher: It is. I am the jewel of the Delta.

Animal Wisdom:

___ _____ _____ _____
_____ __ _____ __
___ _____ __ ____
_____

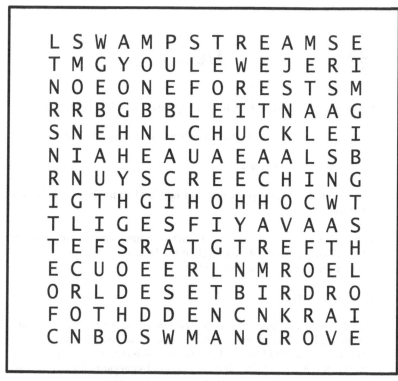

```
L  S  W  A  M  P  S  T  R  E  A  M  S  E
T  M  G  Y  O  U  L  E  W  E  J  E  R  I
N  O  E  O  N  E  F  O  R  E  S  T  S  M
R  R  B  G  B  B  L  E  I  T  N  A  A  G
S  N  E  H  N  L  C  H  U  C  K  L  E  I
N  I  A  H  E  A  U  A  E  A  A  L  S  B
R  N  U  Y  S  C  R  E  E  C  H  I  N  G
I  G  T  H  G  I  H  O  H  H  O  C  W  T
T  L  I  G  E  S  F  I  Y  A  V  A  A  S
T  E  F  S  R  A  T  G  T  R  E  F  T  H
E  C  U  O  E  E  R  L  N  M  R  O  E  L
O  R  L  D  E  S  E  T  B  I  R  D  R  O
F  O  T  H  D  D  E  N  C  N  K  R  A  I
C  N  B  O  S  W  M  A  N  G  R  O  V  E
```

Africa	Estuaries	Morning
Beautiful	Forests	Orange
Bird	Green	Reeds
Blue	Heart	Screeching
Bogs	Hover	Streams
Charming	Jewel	Swamps
Chuckle	Kingfisher	Water
Colors	Malachite	Yellow
Delta	Mangrove	
Duet	Metallic	

Deer

This young deer came and lay next to my house on a hot summer day.

Lauren: You came to rest against my house and I gave you water.

Deer: Thank you. It was hot.

Lauren: May I ask why you came and laid next to the house? It is very unusual.

Deer: I felt safe. You have a special energy around your house. Animals know that it is a safe place to rest and to be around. We do not usually seek people out, we are very cautious.

Lauren: Why is that?

Deer: When people come and build their buildings, the energy of the land changes. It looks and feels different. The vibrations are usually lower. If I look at the land here on this mountain, it has a vibrant energy. This means it is healthy, living. It is the color of living earth. There is a sense of harmony in this color. This harmony is represented by a certain shade to me. When people clear the land of the trees, the vibration changes, the colors change. To me, many places on the mountain look like an energy patchwork of different colors. It has to do with what has been done with the land, and those who live on it. Most people are kind to the land and to us. But some are not.

Animal Wisdom:

‗ ‗ ‗ ‗ ‗ ‗ ‗ ‗ ‗ ‗ ‗ ‗ ‗ ‗ ‗
‗ ‗ ‗ ‗ ‗ ‗ ‗ ‗ ‗ ‗ ‗ ‗ ‗ ‗ ‗ ‗ ‗
‗ ‗ ‗ ‗ ‗ ‗ ‗ ‗ ‗ ‗ ‗ ‗ ‗ ‗ ‗ ‗ ‗ ‗ ‗ ‗

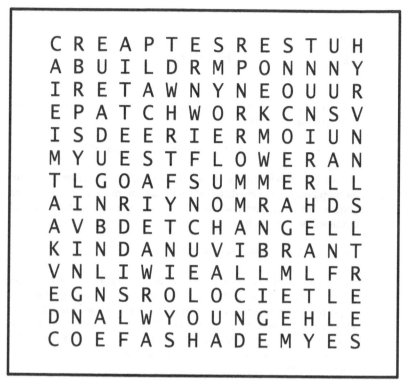

```
C R E A P T E S R E S T U H
A B U I L D R M P O N N N Y
I R E T A W N Y N E O U U R
E P A T C H W O R K C N S V
I S D E E R I E R M O I U N
M Y U E S T F L O W E R A N
T L G O A F S U M M E R L L
A I N R I Y N O M R A H D S
A V B D E T C H A N G E L L
K I N D A N U V I B R A N T
V N L I W I E A L L M L F R
E G N S R O L O C I E T L E
D N A L W Y O U N G E H L E
C O E F A S H A D E M Y E S
```

Animals	Kind	Special
Build	Land	Summer
Cautious	Living	Trees
Change	Lower	Unusual
Colors	Mountain	Vibrant
Deer	Patchwork	Vibration
Different	Places	Water
Energy	Rest	Young
Harmony	Safe	
Healthy	Shade	

Hippos

I talked to a small family of hippos lying on the edge of a waterhole while in a game park in South Africa.

Lauren: How do you feel about being in this environment?

Hippo: We love it here. It's safe and peaceful and also rather beautiful. Our hippo energy is very different than many animals. In a way, we are a bridge between land and water animals. We can easily live and communicate with both. This is unique.

Lauren: Very. Where do humans fit in?

Hippo: Humans come in many kinds. Helpers, Keepers, and Destroyers (poachers). Keepers are those who live and work among us. Helpers are people like you who love animals and want to understand more. The Destroyers, well this is obvious, I think. They see animals as a source to fill their own needs. Of course, these needs are not something animals understand. We cannot and do not understand why Destroyers do what they do.

Lauren: It is hard even for Helpers and Keepers to understand.

Hippo: It's almost as if the Destroyers are their own species, living in a world that is of their own creation. I suppose we all see the world in our own way. We choose to see beauty and try to be in harmony and peace. We wish that for you, too.

Animal Wisdom:

___ _____ ____ ___

_____ _____

_____ __ ____

_____ _____

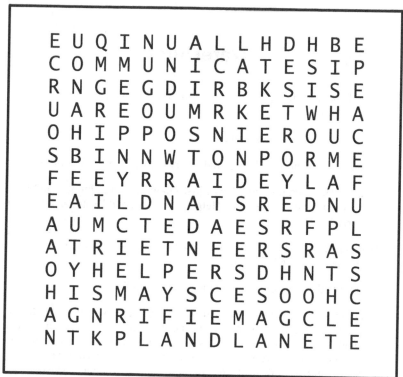

```
E U Q I N U A L L H D H B E
C O M M U N I C A T E S I P
R N G E G D I R B K S I S E
U A R E O U M R K E T W H A
O H I P P O S N I E R O U C
S B I N N W T O N P O R M E
F E E Y R R A I D E Y L A F
E A I L D N A T S R E D N U
A U M C T E D A E S R F P L
A T R I E T N E E R S R A S
O Y H E L P E R S D H N T S
H I S M A Y S C E S O O H C
A G N R I F I E M A G C L E
N T K P L A N D L A N E T E
```

Beauty	Helpers	Safe
Bridge	Hippos	Source
Choose	Human	Species
Communicate	Keepers	Understand
Creation	Kinds	Unique
Destroyers	Land	Waterhole
Family	Needs	Wish
Game	Park	World
Harmony	Peaceful	

Waterbuck

After I spoke with the hippos about humans, I had this conversation with a beautiful waterbuck antelope.

Lauren: We want to admire you.

Waterbuck: Thank you. I am proud of my horns. They are beautiful.

Lauren: They certainly are. I was just talking to some hippos, and they spoke about people as being Helpers, Keepers, and Destroyers. Do you agree?

Waterbuck: Yes, and we teach our young about this too. It helps us explain that people are all different. Some good, some bad.

Lauren: Is there an equivalent in the animal world?

Waterbuck: No, no. Even those of us who are eaten by others think that we are killed for a purpose. The need to survive is very basic, and fundamental to life. It is not destruction; it is life-giving. Humans, we are not so sure. We think that they enjoy the destruction and killing sometimes. But then others are Keepers and Helpers. Most of the people who come here are like that, but not all.

Lauren: Especially the humans who come at night, the poachers.

Waterbuck: Yes, I speak of them. Destroyers. Their hearts are black.

Lauren: Yes, we know of these people and try to stop them.

Waterbuck: Thank you. We will find a way to survive, or not. Until then we try to walk together lightly on the earth. I encourage you to do the same.

Animal Wisdom:

—— —————————— —————
—————— ——— ————
———————— —— ——— ——————

Cristina Smith and Rick Smith with Lauren McCall

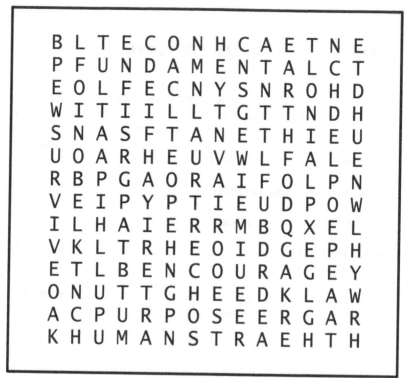

```
B L T E C O N H C A E T N E
P F U N D A M E N T A L C T
E O L F E C N Y S N R O H D
W I T I I L L T G T T N D H
S N A S F T A N E T H I E U
U O A R H E U V W L F A L E
R B P G A O R A I F O L P N
V E I P Y P T I E U D P O W
I L H A I E R R M B Q X E L
V K L T R H E O I D G E P H
E T L B E N C O U R A G E Y
O N U T T G H E E D K L A W
A C P U R P O S E E R G A R
K H U M A N S T R A E H T H
```

Admire	Explain	Proud
Agree	Fundamental	Purpose
Antelope	Hearts	Stop
Basic	Hippos	Survive
Beautiful	Horns	Teach
Different	Humans	Together
Earth	Life	Walk
Encourage	Lightly	Waterbuck
Equivalent	People	Young

Desert Tortoise

The desert tortoise can live fifty to eighty years. Able to survive a year or more without water, they dig burrows to escape scorching summer heat, bitter winter cold, and as a safe haven from predators. These burrows, usually shared by several, can be more than five feet deep. This particular tortoise wanders the deserts of Mexico.

Lauren: You are an ancient species.

Tortoise: Yes, and we live a long time.

Lauren: Do you have a collective *tortoise wisdom* that you would like to share?

Tortoise: When we walk, we create thunder in the ground. We create a timeless vibration in the earth when we walk.

Lauren: Is that the purpose of your species?

Tortoise: We store within us many memories. Memories of changes in the environment of the earth. We will outlast many species, maybe even humans. We will continue to hold the memories. Our connection to the earth is strong. Slowly we pace the rhythms of life at a steady, steady pace. Not fast, not slow. We provide a consistent vibration walking on the earth. The past and the present are all one to us. One vibration steady and true, walking through time.

Animal Wisdom:

—— —— —— ——   —— —— ——   —— —— —— —— —— ——   —— —— ——   ——
—— —— —— —— —— ——   —— —— —— —— —— —— ——   —— —— ——
—— —— ——   —— —— ——

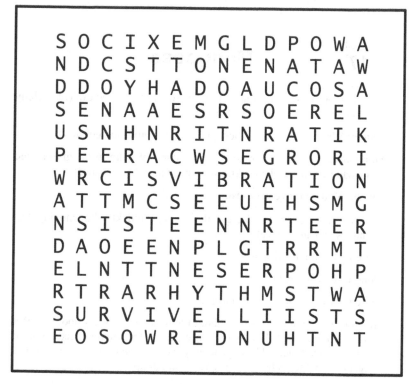

```
S  O  C  I  X  E  M  G  L  D  P  O  W  A
N  D  C  S  T  T  O  N  E  N  A  T  A  W
D  D  O  Y  H  A  D  O  A  U  C  O  S  A
S  E  N  A  A  E  S  R  S  O  E  R  E  L
U  S  N  H  N  R  I  T  N  R  A  T  I  K
P  E  E  R  A  C  W  S  E  G  R  O  R  I
W  R  C  I  S  V  I  B  R  A  T  I  O  N
A  T  T  M  C  S  E  E  U  E  H  S  M  G
N  S  I  S  T  E  E  N  N  R  T  E  E  R
D  A  O  E  E  N  P  L  G  T  R  R  M  T
E  L  N  T  T  N  E  S  E  R  P  O  H  P
R  T  R  A  R  H  Y  T  H  M  S  T  W  A
S  U  R  V  I  V  E  L  L  I  I  S  T  S
E  O  S  O  W  R  E  D  N  U  H  T  N  T
```

Ancient	Mexico	Thunder
Burrows	Outlast	Timeless
Connection	Pace	Tortoise
Consistent	Past	True
Create	Present	Vibration
Desert	Rhythms	Walking
Earth	Species	Wanders
Ground	Store	Wisdom
Haven	Strong	
Memories	Survive	

Mongoose

The mongoose lives in groups of up to fifty called *colonies*. This colony member resides in northern Botswana.

Lauren: What is the role of your species in the environment here?

Mongoose: We keep down some of the pests. We dig in the ground and provide air to the plants. And we represent industriousness.

Lauren: You do move very fast.

Mongoose: Yes, we do. We get things done quickly, but moving fast makes us harder to catch.

Lauren: Do you mean snakes?

Mongoose: Yes, snakes.

Lauren: How you feel about snakes?

Mongoose: Naturally we worry about them, and they worry about us. But we recognize that they, like us, are part of the interconnectedness of life and death here. The dependency we have on each other gives us a respect for each other, and a sense of community.

Lauren: What would you like people to know about you?

Mongoose: We are proud, clever, and industrious. We are loving and we have a strong sense of community. We have families, like you do. We love each other, like you do. And finally, we have a sense of fun. I hope like you do.

Lauren: Sometimes humans can be very serious.

Mongoose: That is a waste. You never know when a snake will come along.

Animal Wisdom:

__ __   ____   _____   _____
_____   __   _____   _____
_____   ____   ____

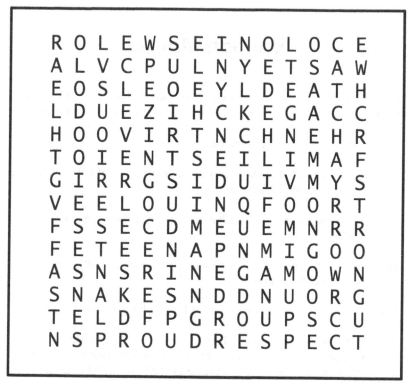

```
R O L E W S E I N O L O C E
A L V C P U L N Y E T S A W
E O S L E O E Y L D E A T H
L D U E Z I H C K E G A C C
H O O V I R T N C H N E H R
T O I E N T S E I L I M A F
G I R R G S I D U I V M Y S
V E E L O U I N Q F O O R T
F S S E C D M E U E M N R R
F E T E E N A P N M I G O O
A S N S R I N E G A M O W N
S N A K E S N D D N U O R G
T E L D F P G R O U P S C U
N S P R O U D R E S P E C T
```

Catch	Hope	Recognize
Clever	Industrious	Respect
Colonies	Life	Role
Communities	Love	Sense
Death	Mongoose	Serious
Dependency	Moving	Snakes
Families	Pests	Strong
Fast	Plants	Waste
Ground	Proud	Worry
Groups	Quickly	

Baboon Mother

Baboons are very social creatures. Did you know that the world's largest monkeys use more than thirty distinct vocalizations to communicate with each other? Groups of baboons are called *troops* and can include dozens to hundreds of community members.

Walking in the bush in Botswana, we watched a troop of baboons having fun and making noise in the trees.

Lauren: You look like you are having fun. Are these your family and friends?

Baboon: Yes. We are very family- and friend-oriented and we enjoy life together. We like to play with each other.

Lauren: Do you have many friends and family that you play with?

Baboon: Of course, very many. Friends are a great joy in life. We laugh, and we play. And we also take care of each other. That is important to all of us. What is good for one is good for all. And what is good for all, is good for one!

Animal Wisdom:

___ ___ ___ ___ ___
___ ___ ____ ___
____ __ _____
_____

```
A S E R U T A E R C L L F O
C N R O N Y L I M A F E A N
S O C I A L T C N I T S I D
D I M P O R T A N T O N E O
F T L M O R W G D A L L M Z
A A M K U S D E R D N U H E
Y Z E T T N T R O O P S E N
S I M O A N I A H G U A L S
T L B H E E R C E B W P Y O
R A E I L E R L A R G E S T
D C R E H T E G O T K S D G
O O S T J O Y S D N E I R F
F V O U B A B O O N L O L Y
A M R G O U N M Y O J N E D
```

Baboon	Friends	Mother
Botswana	Good	Noise
Bush	Great	Oriented
Care	Groups	Play
Communicate	Hundreds	Social
Creatures	Important	Together
Distinct	Largest	Troops
Dozens	Laugh	Vocalizations
Enjoy	Members	
Family	Monkeys	

Muskoka the Horse

People often feel in partnership with their animals, be it emotional or working. Muskoka is a beautiful grey mare who did competition events with her person. I asked Muskoka this question on her person's behalf.

Lauren: We have become even closer and better partners and feel like a strong team together. How can I feel even more *one* with you while we are jumping and riding?

Muskoka: I feel really good about what and how we are doing. In terms of your feeling more like a part of me, well that is a fine idea. Just become a part of me!

Lauren: That's not so easy.

Muskoka: Sure it is. Imagine yourself on my back and your body *sinking* into mine. You will feel my muscles contract as I gather myself, and then lengthen and expand as we jump. I love that idea.

Lauren: I can try that, it does sound fun. Can I do anything else like shifting my weight?

Muskoka: No, I don't think so. Just make sure you anticipate. Look at the jump but not with hard, staring eyes. See it not as something to clear, not as an obstacle. It is something to move through. We should flow over it, like water or wind. It's a soft, unified feeling. Water over a stone in a stream.

Lauren: My goodness, you are poetic today.

Muskoka: Oh yes. I'm deep you know!

Animal Wisdom:

—— —— —— —— ——— —— —— ——— —— —— ——— —— —— ——

—— —— —— ——— —— —— —— —— —— —— —— ——— —— ——

—— —— —— —— —— —— ——— —— —— ——

  *Cristina Smith and Rick Smith with Lauren McCall*

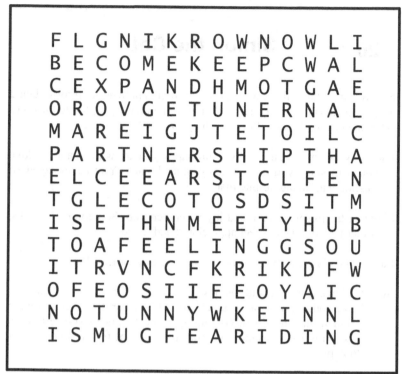

```
F L G N I K R O W N O W L I
B E C O M E K E E P C W A L
C E X P A N D H M O T G A E
O R O V G E T U N E R N A L
M A R E I G J T E T O I L C
P A R T N E R S H I P T H A
E L C E E A R S T C L F E N
T G L E C O T O S D S I T M
I S E T H N M E E I Y H U B
T O A F E E L I N G G S O U
I T R V N C F K R I K D F W
O F E O S I I E E O Y A I C
N O T U N N Y W K E I N N L
I S M U G F E A R I D I N G
```

Become	Horse	Shifting
Body	Imagine	Sinking
Clear	Jump	Soft
Competition	Lengthen	Stone
Contract	Mare	Unified
Emotional	Muscles	Weight
Events	Muskoka	Wind
Expand	Partnership	Working
Feeling	Poetic	
Grey	Riding	

Simon the Cat

Simon is a wonderful cat whose life was quite challenging prior to being adopted by his new family. He settled in well with the people and the other cat in the house. Simon reflects on the power of love.

Lauren: Welcome to our family. I am happy you are with us and we love you. I'm sorry you had so many other homes. You have stayed so trusting and loving despite that.

Simon: I try to spread love and joy wherever I go. Sometimes it works, sometimes not. Here I feel appreciated and loved.

Lauren: That's great. What have you learned in your travels?

Simon: I have learned about the power of love and the impact it has, not only on others, but on yourself too. It's clear that being loving can transform others. But continuing to be loving to yourself when life is hard can sustain you and make it better. It keeps your outlook positive.

Lauren: That is so true. You are an amazing cat.

Simon: I don't know about that but thank you.

Animal Wisdom:

— — — — — — — — — — — — — — — — — — —
— — — — — — — — — — — — — — — — — —
— — — — — — — — — — — — — — — — —
— — — — — —

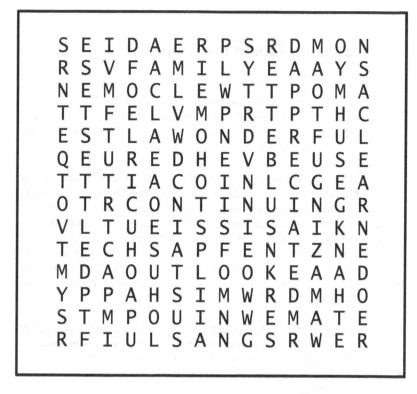

```
S E I D A E R P S R D M O N
R S V F A M I L Y E A A Y S
N E M O C L E W T T P O M A
T T F E L V M P R T P T H C
E S T L A W O N D E R F U L
Q E U R E D H E V B E U S E
T T T I A C O I N L C G E A
O T R C O N T I N U I N G R
V L T U E I S S I S A I K N
T E C H S A P F E N T Z N E
M D A O U T L O O K E A A D
Y P P A H S I M W R D M H O
S T M P O U I N W E M A T E
R F I U L S A N G S R W E R
```

Adopted	Impact	Spread
Amazing	Learned	Sustain
Appreciated	Love	Thank
Better	Outlook	Transform
Clear	Positive	Travels
Continuing	Power	True
Family	Reflects	Trusting
Happy	Settled	Welcome
Home	Simon	Wonderful

Can We *Really* Talk to the Animals?

Dr. Doolittle's dream of talking to the animals is one many of us share. There are psychics who specialize in talking to pets. There are horse, dog, and cat whisperers, and animal communicators. Many of us wonder if animal communication can be learned. Is it some kind of super power available only to a select few?

I had that question too. I took one of Lauren's classes to find out for myself. The answer is yes. It can be learned. You don't even have to believe in animal communication for it to work, just in the possibility of animal communication. Each person in this beginning class was taught a simple technique and successfully communicated with an animal they had never met before who was related to another person in the class. How was that proven? The students asked the animals questions that only they or their human could know the answer to. Like everything else, some are more naturally talented at this than others.

With practice, persistence, and patience, we can become interspecies communicators. No special talents are necessary. Young, old, introverted, extroverted, talkative, or quiet, we all have the potential ability to connect directly. All that is needed is a respect for animals and an authentic, heartfelt desire to connect.

One thing to remember is to talk to the animals. If you do, they will talk back to you. But if you don't talk to the animals, they won't talk back to you, then you won't understand, and when you don't understand you will fear, and when you fear you will destroy the animals, and if you destroy the animals, you will destroy yourself. —Chief Dan George

This inward, personal approach is quite satisfying. In the outside world, recent advances in artificial intelligence (AI) and machine learning suggest that the longstanding dream of being able to converse with animals in a more advanced manner will soon be a reality.

With the help of AI, scientists are learning how to translate animals' vocalizations and facial expressions into something we can understand. A recently developed system listens in on marmoset monkeys to parse the dozen calls they use to communicate with each other in order to assign meaning to each. Another reads sheep's faces to determine whether an animal is in pain and conveys that information to a rancher.

Once ever-evolving and advancing AI is added to the mix, it begins to be clear that the sky is the limit. We probably cannot imagine at this moment what changes in communication, translation, and interaction will happen over the next ten years. Perhaps when revealed, the secret lives of animals will bring forth a new era of interspecies partnerships. Won't it be fun and fascinating to find out?

Mongoose Mother

Another member of a Botswana banded mongoose colony reflects on the essence of interspecies life on earth.

Lauren: What do you find beautiful?

Mongoose: My babies. The love of our community. The gentle way we cuddle together when it is cold. The way we love and care for each other when we are sick. We are a community that cares for each other from birth to death. I find this whole process beautiful.

Lauren: I do too. Do you have community among all species here?

Mongoose: Let's say we are "friendly" rather than friends. This is okay. But the trees, the bushes, and the earth itself, they are the true friends. We are all family in a way. Different branches of the same family.

Lauren: I agree and believe that is true. We must treat each other kindly and with respect.

Mongoose: Yes. Who is to say who is more important than another? Are the trees more important than the sky? No. Is the lion more important than the mongoose? No. We all have our part to play.

Animal Wisdom:

__ ___ _____ ____

_____ ___

_____ _____ ___

_____ _____

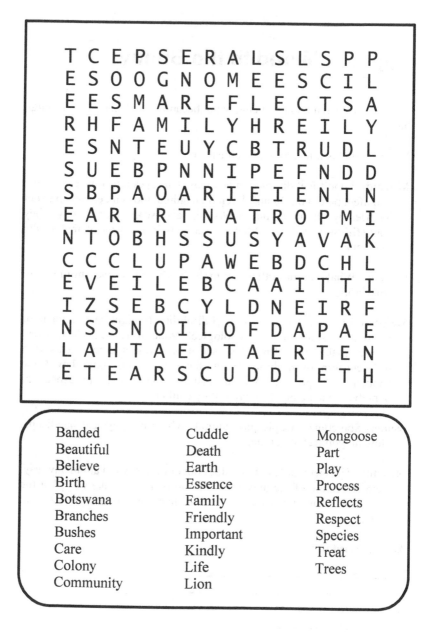

```
T C E P S E R A L S L S P P
E S O O G N O M E E S C I L
E E S M A R E F L E C T S A
R H F A M I L Y H R E I L Y
E S N T E U Y C B T R U D L
S U E B P N N I P E F N D D
S B P A O A R I E I E N T N
E A R L R T N A T R O P M I
N T O B H S S U S Y A V A K
C C C L U P A W E B D C H L
E V E I L E B C A A I T T I
I Z S E B C Y L D N E I R F
N S S N O I L O F D A P A E
L A H T A E D T A E R T E N
E T E A R S C U D D L E T H
```

Banded	Cuddle	Mongoose
Beautiful	Death	Part
Believe	Earth	Play
Birth	Essence	Process
Botswana	Family	Reflects
Branches	Friendly	Respect
Bushes	Important	Species
Care	Kindly	Treat
Colony	Life	Trees
Community	Lion	

22 Meredith the Bunny

Meredith is a remarkable being who became blind part way through her life.

Lauren: What is it like to not be able to see?

Meredith: I don't feel disabled in any way. Our eyes are connected to the judgment part of our brains. Even if an animal looks nice, they may not be friendly. If an animal looks big and scary to a bunny, they may still be very kind. What we see gets in the way of feeling the true being.

Lauren: What about other animals with what we might call "disabilities"?

Meredith: Everyone has some kind of disability. It might be emotional, or physical, or spiritual, or psychological. None of us are perfect. A bad temper makes us selfish, less sensitive towards others. This is a different form of disability. We all have something, some flaw. Mine happens to be physical. We all must overcome, deal with aspects of ourselves that are not as good as they could be.

Lauren: Sometimes people pity animals who have physical handicaps. How do you feel about that?

Meredith: The fact that I am blind does not diminish who I am in any way. I am a creature of the universe. The forms that we take vary, but the seed that is common within us implies that we are all connected and equal.

Animal Wisdom:

———— ——————————
———————————— —— ——
————————— ———
—————————

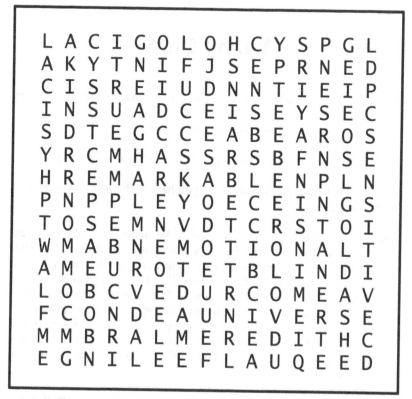

```
L A C I G O L O H C Y S P G L
A K Y T N I F J S E P R N E D
C I S R E I U D N N T I E I P
I N S U A D C E I S E Y S E C
S D T E G C C E A B E A R O S
Y R C M H A S S R S B F N S E
H R E M A R K A B L E N P L N
P N P P L E Y O E C E I N G S
T O S E M N V D T C R S T O I
W M A B N E M O T I O N A L T
A M E U R O T E T B L I N D I
L O B C V E D U R C O M E A V
F C O N D E A U N I V E R S E
M M B R A L M E R E D I T H C
E G N I L E E F L A U Q E E D
```

Aspects	Eyes	Psychological
Being	Feeling	Remarkable
Blind	Flaw	Scary
Brains	Judgment	Seed
Bunny	Kind	Sensitive
Common	Meredith	Spiritual
Connected	Nice	Temper
Disabled	Overcome	True
Emotional	Perfect	Universe
Equal	Physical	

23   Young Buck

Many deer come around my house. This young buck is a frequent visitor.

Lauren: Are you one of the deer who eats my roses?

Buck: Of course! We know you don't like it, but they are so tasty.

Lauren: What kind of relationship do you have with other animal species in this area?

Buck: Deer get along with all creatures. We have no predators except coyotes and they can only hurt us when we are very sick or old. Then sometimes the coyotes give us a quick and easy death. The hawks and falcons also feast on us when we have died. But aside from that, we are friends to animals of different species. We see a lot of beauty and we usually feel a lot of freedom. But our territory is shrinking and we feel uncertainty too. Before, we could forage in the valley below. It was warmer down there in the winter. Now there are more houses and people and less food. I think an essential life skill is learning to cope with change.

Lauren: The world is changing and many species are being crowded out. However, more and more people are looking to connect with the animals in the world around them.

Buck: What people forget is that we are already connected.

Animal Wisdom:

— — —   — — — — — — — — — — —   — — — — —
— — — — — —   — — — — —   — —   — — — — — —   — —
— — — — — —

```
C O N N E C T O D U G P D R
Y P A K C U B E C N R T O O
S I N E N C A E I E C E O T
A H S I R T H K D O V R F N
E S S E H A N A E G A R O F
W N W I T I T T N T L I S H
O O T A R O B M N G L T E T
H I A H R E Y E O R E O S R
S T S S S M U O A D Y R U O
K A T H E Q E L C U E Y O S
W L Y P E U S R A D T E H E
A E A R V I S I T O R Y R S
H R F P T R E T N I W T O F
C H F A L C O N S T S A E F
G N U O Y A N Q U I C K G E
```

Area	Food	Shrinking
Beauty	Forage	Tasty
Buck	Freedom	Territory
Change	Frequent	Valley
Connect	Hawks	Visitor
Coyotes	Houses	Warmer
Death	Predators	Winter
Easy	Quick	Young
Falcons	Relationship	
Feast	Roses	

Orejas the Cat

Orejas is a Scottish Fold who changed his name. Because of the small, folded-over ears typical of his breed, his full name was originally *Sin Orejas*, which means *without ears* in Spanish.

Orejas: I have ears. I prefer to be called Orejas, or just *ears*. I don't want to perpetuate this idea that I don't have ears. I do. They are just different. My name gives the other cats something to tease me about.

Lauren: Of course, I see what you mean.

Orejas: We animals have preferences, perspectives, and opinions too. We are not above, nor below humans. We are different, unique. We are bestowed with our own gifts, evolutionary and spiritual paths. There is a lot of basic wisdom that we can share with people. Animals are, for example, masters of being balanced mentally. Much more so than people, I think.

Lauren: I think people can be balanced and not balanced. We all are different, just as animals are all different.

Animal Wisdom:

___ ___ ___   ___ ___ ___ ___ ___ ___ ___ ___ ___ ___   ___ ___ ___ ___ ___

___ ___ ___   ___ ___ ___ ___ ___   ___ ___ ___ ___   ___ ___ ___ ___ ___ ___   ___ ___

___ ___ ___ ___ ___

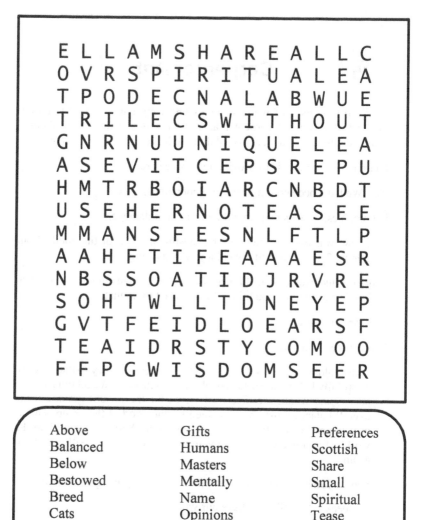

```
E L L A M S H A R E A L L C
O V R S P I R I T U A L E A
T P O D E C N A L A B W U E
T R I L E C S W I T H O U T
G N R N U U N I Q U E L E A
A S E V I T C E P S R E P U
H M T R B O I A R C N B D T
U S E H R N O T E A S E E
M M A N S F E S N L F T L P
A A H F T I F E A A A E S R
N B S S O A T I D J R V R E
S O H T W L L T D N E Y E P
G V T F E I D L O E A R S F
T E A I D R S T Y C O M O O
F F P G W I S D O M S E E R
```

Above	Gifts	Preferences
Balanced	Humans	Scottish
Below	Masters	Share
Bestowed	Mentally	Small
Breed	Name	Spiritual
Cats	Opinions	Tease
Different	Orejas	Unique
Ears	Paths	Wisdom
Evolutionary	Perpetuate	Without
Fold	Perspectives	

Carpenter Ant

I noticed little piles of wood shavings under my patio, made by a long-established colony of carpenter ants. Rather than exterminate them, I addressed the queen ant and asked them to leave of their own accord.

Lauren: Your colony is destroying my space here.

Ant: We have been coming here for generations.

Lauren: Yes, it looks that way; there is a lot of damage.

Ant: That was not our intention, but nesting here is for the good of our colony. The survival of the colony is everything.

Lauren: I understand that. But because of the damage, either you leave or I will have to have you killed. I don't want to do that.

Ant: Are you sure?

Lauren: Yes, I'm sorry.

Ant: The colony must survive. Completing this cycle is key to that. We are a carefully balanced world. We all must contribute. We all must do our part. Some would sacrifice themselves for the greater good, but the overall balance must be maintained for the good of the group. This is near the end of the time when our young are born and come into the world. If you leave us to complete this cycle, then we will not return again.

Lauren: If you can keep your word, then I will happily agree to this.

Ant: I speak for us all. You have our word.

Animal Wisdom:

__ __ __ __ __ __ __ __ __ __ __ __ __ __ __

__ __ __ __ __ __ __ __ __ __ __ __ __ __ __ __ __ __

__ __ __ __ __ __ __ __ __ __ __ __

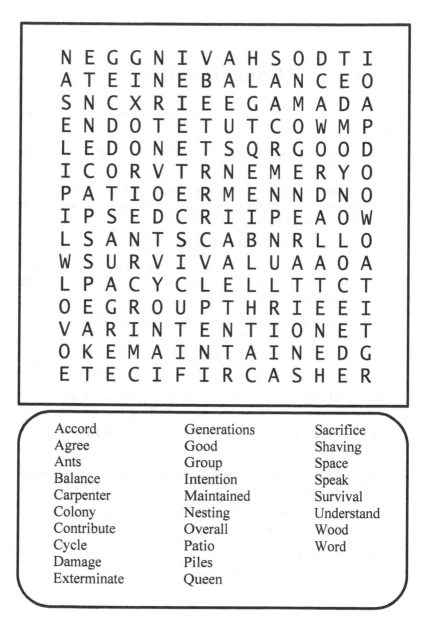

```
N E G G N I V A H S O D T I
A T E I N E B A L A N C E O
S N C X R I E E G A M A D A
E N D O T E T U T C O W M P
L E D O N E T S Q R G O O D
I C O R V T R N E M E R Y O
P A T I O E R M E N N D N O
I P S E D C R I I P E A O W
L S A N T S C A B N R L L O
W S U R V I V A L U A A O A
L P A C Y C L E L L T T C T
O E G R O U P T H R I E E I
V A R I N T E N T I O N E T
O K E M A I N T A I N E D G
E T E C I F I R C A S H E R
```

Accord	Generations	Sacrifice
Agree	Good	Shaving
Ants	Group	Space
Balance	Intention	Speak
Carpenter	Maintained	Survival
Colony	Nesting	Understand
Contribute	Overall	Wood
Cycle	Patio	Word
Damage	Piles	
Exterminate	Queen	

26   Contented Cow

Not far from my home is a herd of cattle. I was curious about something so I spoke to one of them.

Lauren: What do you think about the fact that you are going to be eaten for food?

Cow: We don't worry about it. We don't think about it. There's no point. We can only enjoy the life that we have. It's nice here, we have enough to eat and grass to graze on.

Lauren: What would you like people to know about cows and your life?

Cow: We feel proud to be cows. However, all animals deserve to have some dignity. Just because you eat us doesn't mean that you can be cruel or abusive.

Lauren: I suppose you would encourage people to eat animals who have lived good, contented lives.

Cow: Of course. Sadness, fear—they create vibrations within the body. When people eat unhappy animals, they ingest unhappy meat.

Lauren: Unfortunately, people do not often know where their food comes from. Many people live far from where food is grown or raised.

Cow: That makes me a little bit sad for them. They don't know what they are eating.

Lauren: That is how many people live now. It is often an impersonal relationship with food.

Cow: Then, before they eat, they should seek to neutralize the vibrations of what they are eating.

Animal Wisdom:

__ __ ____ __ ___ _____
___ ___ _____ ___ __
____ __ ___ ___

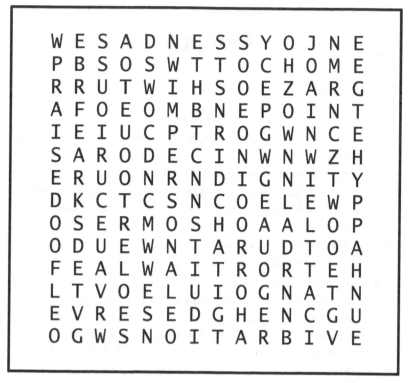

```
W E S A D N E S S Y O J N E
P B S O S W T T O C H O M E
R R U T W I H S O E Z A R G
A F O E O M B N E P O I N T
I E I U C P T R O G W N C E
S A R O D E C I N W N W Z H
E R U O N R N D I G N I T Y
D K C T C S N C O E L E W P
O S E R M O S H O A A L O P
O D U E W N T A R U D T O A
F E A L W A I T R O R T E H
L T V O E L U I O G N A T N
E V R E S E D G H E N C G U
O G W S N O I T A R B I V E
```

Cattle	Fear	Neutralize
Contented	Food	Nice
Cows	Good	Point
Cruel	Grass	Proud
Curious	Graze	Raised
Deserve	Grown	Sadness
Dignity	Home	Unhappy
Eaten	Impersonal	Vibrations
Encourage	Ingest	
Enjoy	Meat	

Octopus

This perceptive, mystical octopus lives alone in a small tank in a Tokyo aquarium.

Lauren: What would you like me to know about you?

Octopus: That I can think and feel. That places like this depress my life force and vibration.

Lauren: And what are you learning in this lifetime?

Octopus: I have wondered about that myself. It's hard to imagine that there is a purpose to this existence, but I think that I am experiencing a very reflective life.

Lauren: Inwardly reflective you mean?

Octopus: Yes. Nothing else to do but reflect.

Lauren: Do you watch the people?

Octopus: No. People are not interesting to me. Very few people come to the glass with a feeling of empathy. They usually comment on my size, as though being big is some kind of achievement. It's as though I'm in my own world. But I guess it is what drives me inward. Inner worlds, inner journeys.

Lauren: That has great value.

Octopus: It does. But I need to find a context for it all. I am me, but in relation to what?

Lauren: Your past lives? Creation itself?

Octopus: Yes, perhaps. I guess there really isn't any other meaningful way to look at it.

Lauren: In human terms, we have people who retreat from the world into lives of silence and contemplation.

Octopus: Then this would be the equivalent.

Animal Wisdom:

— — — — — — — — — — — — — — — — —
— — — — — — — — — — — —
— — — — — — — — — — — — — — — — — —
— — —

```
S Y E N R U O J S I M L E N C
E E Q V N O I T A L E R R E V
E F U A A L S A Q U A R I U M
N O I T A L P M E T N O C A N
D N V L R U U L V H I R E T R
G L A S S E P E I I N V C O E
U I L R E O F Y T N G I N C N
S M E T E O H L P K F B E T N
H A N P R T A D E E U R L O I
E G T C A C E R C C L A I P W
X I E P I P T A R F T T S U O
T N M T R O R W E E A I A S R
O E S E K R D N P E I O V N L
A Y S Y R Y I I R L N N N E D
M S O E R Y O C O N T E X T U
```

Aquarium	Imagine	Reflective
Contemplation	Inner	Relation
Context	Inwardly	Silence
Creation	Journeys	Think
Depress	Life	Tokyo
Empathy	Meaningful	Value
Equivalent	Mystical	Vibration
Feel	Octopus	World
Force	People	
Glass	Perceptive	

Oso the Dog

I talked to young Oso at a shelter after Hurricane Katrina. The placement specialists did their best to find just the right homes for the animals taken in after the disaster.

Lauren: What do you think of this shelter? Everyone here is doing their best for you.

Oso: Well in some ways it's better than where I was. I'd still like to be somebody's special dog.

Lauren: We would like to find you a new person or a new family, too. It would help us to know, what kind of a home would you like?

Oso: Right now, I just want to be loved and wanted. I want people who will take me places. I see other dogs in cars. I could go places with my people. I would like that.

Lauren: Wonderful. What kinds of things do you like to do?

Oso: I'll do anything, run, walk, play, I don't mind.

Lauren: Okay. Do you like kids?

Oso: Whew. That depends on the kids. Maybe a nice kid to play with? Yes, that might be nice. I guess I just want to be loved.

Lauren: Please know that you are very loved. And think of this place as a stopping spot on your way to your new forever home.

Animal Wisdom:

— — — — — — — — — — — — — — — — —
— — — — — — — — — — — — — —

```
E C I N E S E M O H V E S R
H S R S A N Y T H I N G R E
U P Y E W A L K O S N E A T
R O L C F W N K B A G N C S
R T W A T I I I S E T O W A
I R A L C D N Y R O T O D S
C E N P S E L D S T N T P I
A T T B E I M D N D A E E D
N L E L M R N E E O C K E R
E E D A I E Y R N I S V O V
T H F G P O F A A T O R E D
S S H E U U A L L L N D E W
E T D N L S T O P P I N G P
B A G N T E F O R E V E R D
```

Anything	Homes	Right
Best	Hurricane	Shelter
Better	Katrina	Special
Cars	Kids	Spot
Depends	Loved	Stopping
Disaster	Nice	Walk
Dogs	Person	Wanted
Family	Placement	Wonderful
Find	Places	Young
Forever	Play	

Sanctuary Elephant

Research shows that elephants are as intelligent as chimps and dolphins. In addition to their highly developed brains, elephants' trunks are truly remarkable. These prehensile noses house the largest number of genes dedicated to smell of any mammal. Elephants have the best sense of smell in the animal kingdom. They have millions of receptor cells contained in the upper nasal cavity and can detect water sources up to twelve miles away. At a sanctuary in South Africa, the elephants are asked by their keepers to walk with visitors while allowing them to hold on to their trunks. I asked this elephant about those walks.

Lauren: What do you think of doing this with people?

Elephant: This makes me feel a bit silly, but it's nice that people want to walk with me. I am learning about different species. Maybe I'm supposed to take what I learn about people to the next place where I go and then share it.

Animal Wisdom:

__ __ __ __ __   __ __ __ __ __ __   __ __ __

__ __ __ __ __ __   __ __   __ __ __ __

__ __ __ __ __ __ __ __   __ __ __ __ __ __

__ __ __ __ __

```
T H T U O S N I A R B O N H
U L C H A L C S W C L O O W
S E L A S A N A M A I L S L
L A D E V E L O P E D R E B
M R E I E K I H R S L N F C
I N T E L L I G E N T L H A
L Y E C G G R S H I T I V O
L F C E H K E E E H M Y I E
I L T L S E T C N P L O S N
O G Y L E E A N S L E C I T
N E E S N P W D I O B E T Y
S O N N S E D S L D W O O R
S H A R E R E C E P T O R D
T R U N K S S P E C I E S S
```

Africa	Hold	Share
Brains	Intelligent	Silly
Cavity	Keepers	Smell
Cells	Learn	South
Chimps	Millions	Species
Detect	Nasal	Trunks
Developed	Nose	Visitors
Dolphins	Prehensile	Walk
Genes	Receptor	Water
Highly	Sense	

Sanctuary Elephant (continued)

Lauren: What would you say to elephants about people?

Elephant: There is a lot of kindness from people. It's nice that they want to be close to us and to support us. But I know very well there are plenty of people out there who want to exploit us and kill us. I guess there are good people and bad.

Lauren: How do you tell the difference?

Elephant: Elephants spend most of our time feeling the vibration of the earth. And of course, we try to read your intent. We are good at adapting according to changes in weather, food, and present dangers. But there are changes it seems we cannot avoid. We cannot see them and we cannot feel them until it is too late. Perhaps I'm here to learn more about what the vibrations are so that I can better identify them to others when I get back into the wild. I wonder if it will make a difference. In the end, I don't think it will. But we must survive, or try to. The vibration of the earth is changing so fast. I do not know if it is something that we can stop or slow down. Can we adapt or change fast enough?

Lauren: I hope so.

Animal Wisdom:

___ ___ ___ ___   ___ ___ ___   ___ ___ ___ ___ ___   ___ ___ ___
___ ___ ___ ___ ___   ___ ___   ___   ___ ___ ___ ___ ___ ___ ___ ___ ___
___ ___ ___   ___ ___ ___   ___ ___ ___ ___ ___ ___ ___

```
T N E T N I C L F P O F V P
E A H O P E N L O O E D E T
R F E A T T P T O E O O I S
H A E W D R S L L S P D W S
P S O L I R E I E L E O E E
R T I L F D N H E N N A A N
E W S S F G A S T D T V R D
S E E R E A D I E A I Y T N
E V G A R N F R C B E T H I
N I N U E Y A R R Y F W O K
T V A E N Y R A U T C N A S
S R H R C A T S R E G N A D
L U C L E I A D A P T I N G
O S L S O T N A H P E L E P
W E C N T R O P P U S I E S
```

Adapting	Hope	Slow
Changes	Identify	Stop
Close	Intent	Support
Dangers	Kindness	Survive
Difference	Nice	Vibration
Earth	People	Weather
Elephant	Plenty	Wild
Fast	Present	Wonder
Feeling	Read	
Food	Sanctuary	

The Puzzle of Intelligence

In order to consider the question of animal intelligence, we first want to look at intelligence in general. The way we define human intelligence has changed dramatically in the last fifty years. Perspective has shifted. It used to be that either you were good at reading, writing, and arithmetic, or you weren't smart at all. We now know that intelligence comes in all different flavors, like ice cream. And the butter pecans are just as valid as the mint chocolate chips and vanillas. Gone is the belief that if we were not good at logic or language, we weren't very smart.

The shift happened in the early 1980s when Harvard University professor and developmental psychologist Howard Gardener unveiled his landmark Multiple Intelligences theory. He defined several types of human smart. Each individual is a unique blend of them, which makes each of us uniquely intelligent.

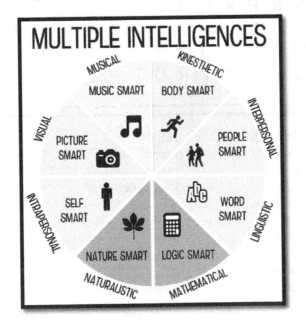

Our primary intelligences often reflect our natural tendencies, though we are not limited to just those. We can learn and nurture others within ourselves. Determination and will are always factors. Surprise! We are as diverse in our intelligence and ways of expressing it as we are in our cultures, religions, belief systems, and work preferences. Who knew?

Think about the people you know. How many of them do you consider smart? Or even brilliant? Is it all in the same way? Know any mechanical geniuses? Amazing athletes? Extraordinary musicians? Inspirational teachers? More and more we are coming to understand that the power of consciousness and ability comes from our diversity. Our special talents guide us and enrich all of humanity, not only our individual lives. Isn't that awesome?

And then there is animal intelligence.

We tend to consider all of the other diverse species on earth with the same intelligence measure as we do people. Are they as smart as we are? Are they conscious beings? How do they feel? We tend to project our human concepts onto them.

Until fairly recently, animals were considered to be unthinking machines and humans the only truly intelligent species. This obsolete model of quantifying animal intelligence was a hierarchical ranking based on the human criteria of complexity which placed humans at the top. We were smart. They were just "dumb" animals. We know better now.

Based on recent research that allows animals to show their smarts unhindered by human preconception, we have discovered that there may be more similarities between human and animal intelligence than differences. We can't put them on a simple scale, because all animals are very smart in knowing what they need to do to survive. The wolf, hippo, ant, horse, and salamander all have their own unique brilliance based on the circumstances of their lives.

One study reveals that thirty bird species and thirty mammal species share the same pattern of pitch and speed in basic messages. Humans and the other fifty nine species can understand each other when they express aggression, hostility, appeasement, approachability, submission, and fear.

Many modern scientists in diverse disciplines tend to agree that animal intelligence looks like an integrated Tree of Life with our roots in the earth and each branch being a different species.

There are new studies and experiments conducted all the time at sanctuaries, zoos, and aquariums around the world. It turns out that animals are pretty smart in learning human interaction, much more so than humans are at learning interspecies languages. Dolphins can use a touch screen. Chimpanzees, bonobos, gorillas, and orangutans have used sign language, physical tokens, keyboards, and touch screens to communicate. Elephants are painting and playing music. Finally, after decades of study, we are now understanding the elephant language and we can even consult an online elephant language translator. There's talk of an Interspecies Internet being developed. These new technologies, along with integrated artificial intelligence, can enhance and advance our ability to communicate with our other brilliant planet mates.

We live together on our amazing planet, each individual having its own purpose. It takes all of us to keep the balance of the ecosystem. We are all interconnected. We can learn so much from the animals about how to live in harmony and balance on the Earth. Are we humans willing to let go of our prejudice and assumption of superiority? With respect and openness, animals can be seen as equals and potential teachers. Who knows what lines of communication will open up? Maybe we can all benefit and learn something from each other.

Bella the Dog

Egyptian monuments from five thousand years ago have drawings of dogs resembling Great Danes. Early written descriptions of similar dogs were found in Chinese literature circa 1121 BCE. An elderly Great Dane who lives in Mexico, Bella seems to enjoy quiet reflection. I asked her about her inner world.

Lauren: What is the importance of stillness?

Bella: To me, being still is a time when I can most fully be myself. Being still enables me to just be with whatever is happening around me. I can be fully present. I'm not tempted to focus on the random thoughts that may come into my head. If I see a bird, I can notice and enjoy the bird. It flies in and out of my head as fast as it flies past my eyes. Once there, now gone. What remains from the experience is my stillness. This time, though, my being is enhanced with the resonance of the bird.

Animal Wisdom:

_ _ _ _ _ _   _ _ _ _ _   _ _ _ _ _ _ _   _ _
_ _ _ _ _ _   _ _ _ _ _   _ _ _ _ _ _ _   _ _ _
_ _   _ _ _ _   _ _ _ _ _ _

```
O C I X E M Q U N O T I C E
I E A S T H G U O H T T T N
I Y L R E D L E I N N E R J
M E L I T E R A T U R E S O
B R E I N S A P C G S U T Y
S P B E A C L R E R D R I B
F C N R C R I E L E E M L B
O T O A H I M S F S P O L T
C E H N I P I E E O W N N I
U I T D N T S N R N T U E D
S U H O E I P T I A N M S L
E Q A M S O A Y E N N E S R
N D I N E N O R G C U N R O
A C R I C S G N I E B T W W
D O R E N H A N C E D S L D
```

Being	Enjoy	Quiet
Bella	Focus	Random
Bird	Great	Reflection
Chinese	Importance	Resonance
Circa	Inner	Similar
Danes	Literature	Stillness
Descriptions	Mexico	Thoughts
Egyptian	Monuments	World
Elderly	Notice	
Enhanced	Present	

32 Bella the Dog (continued)

The most famous of Great Danes are cartoon characters: Scooby Doo, Marmaduke, and Astro. Known as gentle giants, these dogs were once thought to ward off ghosts and evil spirits. Bella explains more about her perceptions.

Lauren: What do you mean "the resonance of the bird?"

Bella: Let us say that it is a beautiful bird. Then the enjoyment of the colors remains with me, and the enjoyment is something that is felt in the vibration of my being. Or maybe the bird makes a noise, then the echo of that sound is there, if not in my head, then in my spirit that has been elevated by the experience. I suppose the gift of stillness is that it enables you to raise your spirits—your vibration—by noticing and being fully present to the beauty around you.

Lauren: And what about experiences and things that are not beautiful?

Bella: Allow them to slide through your awareness, like a ghost, neither here nor there.

Animal Wisdom:

___ _____ _____

_____ __ ____ __

_____ ____ __ ___

____ _____

```
T H O H C E E E X G Q D U T
I V G H O S T S P I R I T L
S I I E L T N E G A S T E E
E S F B O U U B W N T E C F
A L T L R E F O O T M N B S
E W E A S A L I U S A J U G
T N A V Y L T O T N R O F O
L I O R A P F I O U M Y E D
I A S O E T N S O A A M R E
V D S C T N E O F N D E E A
L A R T E R E D I D U N B W
H E E I R N A S I S K T W E
P H A Y B O O C S L E R E C
A L M W I T D N U O S H I N
```

Allow
Astro
Awareness
Beautiful
Bird
Cartoon
Colors
Dogs
Echo
Elevated

Enjoyment
Famous
Felt
Gentle
Ghosts
Giants
Gift
Head
Marmaduke
Noise

Perceptions
Resonance
Scooby
Slide
Sound
Spirit
Vibration
Ward

Gemsbok Antelope

This stunning male gemsbok lives on a nature reserve in South Africa. He sees many people driving their cars through the reserve, hoping to see animals at every turn.

Lauren: What do you think of all those people stopping to take photos of you?

Gemsbok: Well, I feel admired, I suppose. It's always nice to be admired. Don't people feel that way too?

Lauren: Yes, we do. What do you think is the difference between people and animals?

Gemsbok: Animals take life as they come to it. We think that life comes as it comes and in its own time. It's a bit like the way people drive around here expecting to see certain animals. In reality you come to animals as you come to them. You cannot force them to appear at any given time or place. It is the joy of discovery that is so important.

Lauren: I agree. Sometimes people can try to force things, or have fixed ideas about what they want in life.

Gemsbok: Ah, I see. I think that in life, you must search less and allow yourself to discover more.

Animal Wisdom:

— — —   — — — — — — —   — —
— — — — — — — — — —   — —
— — — — — — — — —   — — — —   — —   — — —
— — — — — —   — — — —   — — — — — — — — —

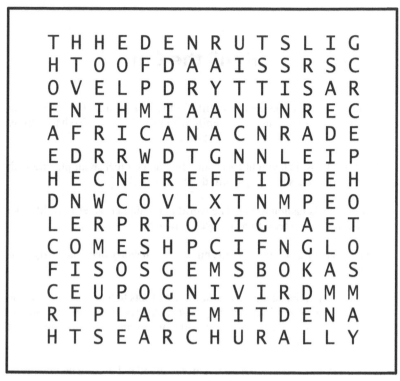

```
T H H E D E N R U T S L I G
H T O O F D A A I S S R S C
O V E L P D R Y T T I S A R
E N I H M I A A N U N R E C
A F R I C A N A C N R A D E
E D R R W D T G N N L E I P
H E C N E R E F F I D P E H
D N W C O V L X T N M P E O
L E R P R T O Y I G T A E T
C O M E S H P C I F N G L O
F I S O S G E M S B O K A S
C E U P O G N I V I R D M M
R T P L A C E M I T D E N A
H T S E A R C H U R A L L Y
```

Admired	Fixed	Photos
Africa	Force	Place
Animals	Gemsbok	Reality
Antelope	Hoping	Reserve
Appear	Ideas	Search
Cars	Important	South
Comes	Life	Stunning
Difference	Male	Time
Discover	Nature	Turn
Driving	People	

Kenji the Cat

Young Kenji lives an enchanted life in the countryside. He has trees to climb, pastures to scour, and a family who loves him. He also has a strong sense of self and what it means to be a cat.

Lauren: I know that you like to hunt. How do you feel about playing with mice or snakes before you kill them?

Kenji: It feels natural to me. The world is my dinner plate! I see life like that too. It is a feast to be enjoyed, savored.

Lauren: That's a nice philosophy, but don't you worry that you terrify your prey?

Kenji: I don't think about it. It is the nature of cats to hunt. I don't examine the philosophy of it all. For me, I just allow myself to follow my nature. It is my inner catness that determines who I am, and how I behave. I really enjoy being a cat.

Lauren: Indeed, but it's not just your catness that defines who you are, it is your individual personality too.

Kenji: That's very true. But I do believe that mice will be mice, and cats will be cats. We both engage in the sacred dance in our own way!

Animal Wisdom:

— — — — — — — —   — — — — — —   — —
— — —   — — — —   — —   —
— — — — — — — — —   — — — — — —   — —
— — —   — — — — —   — —   — — — —

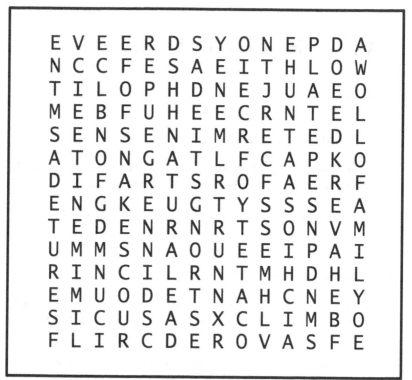

```
E V E E R D S Y O N E P D A
N C C F E S A E I T H L O W
T I L O P H D N E J U A E O
M E B F U H E E C R N T E L
S E N S E N I M R E T E D L
A T O N G A T L F C A P K O
D I F A R T S R O F A E R F
E N G K E U G T Y S S S E A
T E D E N R N R T S O N V M
U M M S N A O U E E I P A I
R I N C I L R N T M H D H L
E M U O D E T N A H C N E Y
S I C U S A S X C L I M B O
F L I R C D E R O V A S F E
```

Behave	Family	Sacred
Catness	Feast	Savored
Climb	Follow	Scour
Countryside	Hunt	Self
Dance	Kenji	Sense
Determines	Mice	Snakes
Dinner	Natural	Strong
Enchanted	Pastures	Trees
Engage	Philosophy	
Examine	Plate	

Blacktip Reef Shark

Now living in a tank in a Tokyo aquarium, this shark was likely taken into captivity off the coast of Okinawa, Japan.

Lauren: Sharks are known as great predators.

Shark: All animals who eat others are predators. We don't kill just for the sake of it. We kill to eat, like all other flesh-eating species.

Lauren: That makes sense. And yet people are usually afraid of sharks.

Shark: That's interesting.

Lauren: How do sharks feel about people in general?

Sharks: I can't speak for sharks in all parts of the world. We are different, but the sharks in this place definitely question people's right to imprison us in this way. The purpose is unclear to us.

Lauren: In this case it is so people can see you and learn more about you.

Shark: The price of that is our freedom. It is an unfair exchange.

Lauren: Yes, it is. Thank you for your perspective.

Animal Wisdom:

__ _ _____ _____ _____ __

____ ___ _____

_____ ___ __ _____

_____ __ ____

```
W E T O K Y O N E V G E R K
N H H O W D W H A N T M W E
W S G I I M P R I S O N L L
U E I A S R O T A D E R P E
N L R P E R S P E C T I V E
F F E E A T E E A N H R G
A O F O R Q R B S P O U G N
I K H E A F U L O T I N O A
R I T S A O C A P I T T H H
U N C L E A R C R V S E R C
I A S E K N J K U I E T O X
F W E G R E A T P T U Y E E
S A U A A N P I T Y Q M I K
L W E E H L A P R I C E O A
L L I K S O N D L R O W K S
```

Afraid	Interesting	Reef
Aquarium	Japan	Right
Blacktip	Kill	Sake
Captivity	Learn	Shark
Coast	Okinawa	Tokyo
Exchange	Perspective	Unclear
Flesh	Predator	Unfair
Freedom	Price	World
Great	Purpose	
Imprison	Question	

Blacktip Reef Shark (continued)

Blacktip reef sharks are apex predators in their own shallow reef ecosystem. Apex predators are at the top of a food chain. No other animals prey upon them. They are vital to their ecosystems and, ultimately, to evolution. By weeding out the slow, weak, and dying animals in the wild, apex predators increase the health of the population as a whole.

Shark: Do you know what sharks call people? Predators. They kill so many of us. I think it depends on your perspective.

Lauren: I agree. Perhaps some of the impressions that people have about you is based on the way you look. Sleek, fast, and with sharp teeth.

Shark: All fish are sleek. It is efficient and necessary to move through water. Our teeth are sharp because of the kind of food we eat. We have to be able to grab and chew through flesh. As a species, we see ourselves as efficient survivors. Humans, in turn, are efficient killers. And we do not capture people and put you in big bowls of water to swim round and round endlessly.

Animal Wisdom:

___ _____ __

_____ __ _____ __

_____

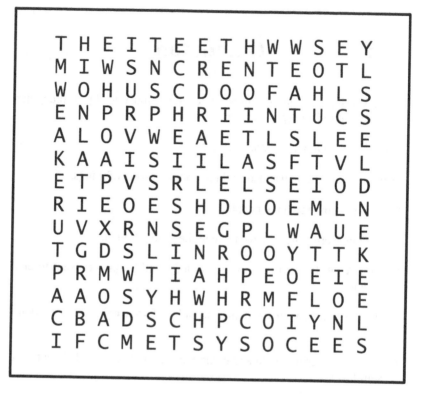

```
T H E I T E E T H W W S E Y
M I W S N C R E N T E O T L
W O H U S C D O O F A H L S
E N P R P H R I I N T U C S
A L O V W E A E T L S L E E
K A A I S I I L A S F T V L
E T P V S R L E L S E I O D
R I E O E S H D U O E M L N
U V X R N S E G P L W A U E
T G D S L I N R O O Y T T K
P R M W T I A H P E O E I E
A A O S Y H W H R M F L O E
C B A D S C H P C O I Y N L
I F C M E T S Y S O C E E S
```

Apex	Food	Slow
Bowls	Grab	Survivors
Capture	Health	Swim
Chain	Impression	Teeth
Chew	Increase	Ultimately
Dying	Population	Vital
Ecosystem	Prey	Weak
Endlessly	Shallow	Whole
Evolution	Sharp	Wild
Fast	Sleek	

37 # Orangutan

While visiting a zoo in the United States, I was intrigued by an orangutan who seemed to be deep in thought.

Lauren: What are you thinking about?

Orangutan: My mind wanders; I think about all sorts of things.

Lauren: Do you watch the people?

Orangutan: Sometimes. I have to be in the mood though.

Lauren: What do you think about people? Would you ever want to be a human?

Orangutan: I envy your freedom. I see a lot of your children. But I don't know....

Lauren: I wonder if people and orangutans are not so very different on a soul level.

Orangutan: Possibly not. We are all here for a reason. In that sense we are all experiencing life and growing. The physical experiences of our species are different from each other. I wonder if our inner experiences are similar though.

Lauren: I think they might be. We experience love, loss, happiness, sadness, and so on. Then we try to learn from all of it.

Animal Wisdom:

— — — —   — — — — — — — —   — — — — — —
— — — — — — — — — —   — — —
— — — — — — — — — —

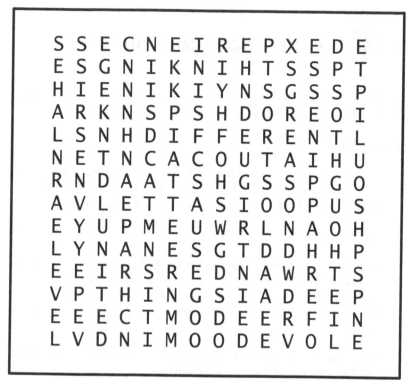

```
S  S  E  C  N  E  I  R  E  P  X  E  D  E
E  S  G  N  I  K  N  I  H  T  S  S  P  T
H  I  E  N  I  K  I  Y  N  S  G  S  S  P
A  R  K  N  S  P  S  H  D  O  R  E  O  I
L  S  N  H  D  I  F  F  E  R  E  N  T  L
N  E  T  N  C  A  C  O  U  T  A  I  H  U
R  N  D  A  A  T  S  H  G  S  S  P  G  O
A  V  L  E  T  T  A  S  I  O  O  P  U  S
E  Y  U  P  M  E  U  W  R  L  N  A  O  H
L  Y  N  A  N  E  S  G  T  D  D  H  H  P
E  E  I  R  S  R  E  D  N  A  W  R  T  S
V  P  T  H  I  N  G  S  I  A  D  E  E  P
E  E  E  C  T  M  O  D  E  E  R  F  I  N
L  V  D  N  I  M  O  O  D  E  V  O  L  E
```

Children	Level	Sorts
Deep	Loss	Soul
Different	Love	States
Envy	Mind	Things
Experiences	Mood	Thinking
Freedom	Orangutan	Thought
Happiness	Physical	United
Inner	Reason	Wanders
Intrigued	Sadness	Watch
Learn	Seemed	

Orangutan (continued)

In Malay, *orang* means person and *utan* is derived from *hutan*, which means forest. This person of the forest shares more thoughts.

Lauren: What are you learning?

Orangutan: That you get out of life what you put into it. Put in happiness, contentment, patience, and you get back love and peacefulness. Resentment and anger give you discontent and impatience.

Lauren: Very wise.

Orangutan: I'm grateful for the experience of being able to learn. You can learn anywhere, in the forest, or even in a zoo. Anywhere. You have to make the most of what you have and take it for the opportunity that it is. A lot of orangutans see life this way, that you get out of it what you put into it.

Lauren: Some people see it that way too. Some people don't. Some people feel that they are entitled to good things.

Orangutan: Good things, bad things, they are everywhere. Notice good, life gets better. Notice bad, life is unpleasant. You get out of it what you put into it.

Lauren: Perfect. Thank you.

Animal Wisdom:

__ __   _____   ___   _____

_____   ____   _____   ___

_____

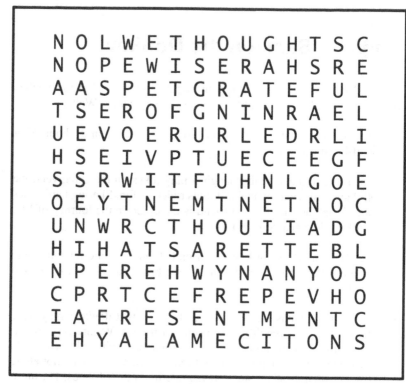

```
N O L W E T H O U G H T S C
N O P E W I S E R A H S R E
A A S P E T G R A T E F U L
T S E R O F G N I N R A E L
U E V O E R U R L E D R L I
H S E I V P T U E C E E G F
S S R W I T F U H N L G O E
O E Y T N E M T N E T N O C
U N W R C T H O U I I A D G
H I H A T S A R E T T E B L
N P E R E H W Y N A N Y O D
C P R T C E F R E P E V H O
I A E R E S E N T M E N T C
E H Y A L A M E C I T O N S
```

Anger	Grateful	Opportunity
Anywhere	Happiness	Peacefulness
Better	Hutan	Perfect
Contentment	Impatience	Person
Entitled	Learning	Resentment
Everywhere	Life	Shares
Feel	Love	Thoughts
Forest	Malay	Wise
Good	Notice	

Samson the Donkey

Samson lives at a donkey sanctuary in England. Donkeys like to socialize with each other. His best friend is another donkey named Walter.

Lauren: Tell me about your friendship with Walter, and about what friendship means to you.

Samson: I like to make Walter laugh. I play jokes on the caregivers; we both laugh. Sharing joy makes things twice as fun. Sharing hard times makes it half as bad. A good friend is a partner on the journey of life. We all need companions and friends.

Lauren: There are different kinds of friends though. Some for fun, some who are perhaps more comforting. Some bring out the best in us, and some the worst.

Samson: Ugh. Humans are so complex. It's true that donkeys may have different friends, even different species of friends. We are very sought after as friends, you know. But really a friend is a being who will guide you, listen to you, support you, and remind you that you are not alone no matter what. Donkeys are always grateful for their friends. The more true friends you have, the more joy you have to share.

Lauren: Thank you, Samson. I'm glad you and Walter have each other.

Samson: Walter is the dandelion in the pasture of my life. Bright and sweet.

Animal Wisdom:

___ _____ ____ _____

___ _____ __ ___

_____

```
T R O P P U S A M S O N O U
S G U I D E G R A T E F U L
R T H G I R B R L Z I V E S
O A B C A R E G I V E R S R
W E E C O M P L E X C E A E
N P S R I M A C J E O N N H
S E T D N I F A O C M T C N
P L D E C O D O U I P R T E
N A S O E P I F R W A A U H
A U S H N W L L N T N P A N
C G E T A K S A E J I D R B
Y H O L U R E H Y D O N Y U
R F T R I R I Y E N N K G D
S E H F R I E N D I S A E P
R S L I S T E N G L A N D S
```

Best	Grateful	Samson
Bright	Guide	Sanctuary
Caregivers	Half	Sharing
Comforting	Jokes	Socialize
Companions	Journey	Species
Complex	Laugh	Support
Dandelion	Listen	Sweet
Donkey	Partner	Twice
England	Pasture	Walter
Friend	Play	Worst

Sea Otter

Native to the northern and eastern Pacific Ocean, sea otters are resourceful and playful. A group on land is called a *romp*. If the community is hanging in the water, it is called a *raft*. This Oregon coastal resident talks about how otters view life.

Lauren: People think otters are fun and playful. Can you tell me about the otter sense of play?

Otter: Life should be fun. Aside from looking out for your physical safety, life should be fun. So, we have play as a priority in our lives. Whether it is chasing each other or dropping things in the water to chase as they sink towards the bottom. There is a sense of play and fun in whatever we enjoy in life.

Lauren: This must keep you happy, give you a positive outlook, and keep your vibration light.

Otter: Otters do have a light vibration. We have the freedom of movement through water. We have speed and lightness. Our physical being is light and quick, and our inner being is quick and light too. If you want to have fun and experience lightness, be an otter!

Animal Wisdom:

__ __ __ __ __ __   __ __ __ __   __ __   __ __   __ __   __

__ __ __ __ __ __   __ __ __ __ __   __ __ __

__ __ __ __ __   __ __   __ __ __ __

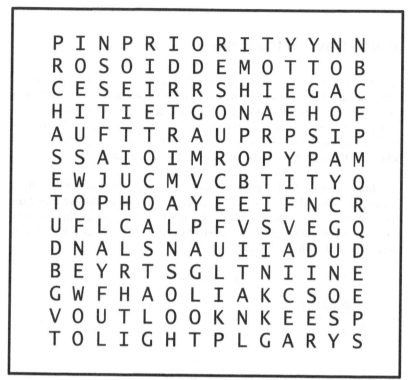

```
P I N P R I O R I T Y Y N N
R O S O I D D E M O T T O B
C E S E I R R S H I E G A C
H I T I E T G O N A E H O F
A U F T T R A U P R P S I P
S S A I O I M R O P Y P A M
E W J U C M V C B T I T Y O
T O P H O A Y E E I F N C R
U F L C A L P F V S V E G Q
D N A L S N A U I I A D U D
B E Y R T S G L T N I I N E
G W F H A O L I A K C S O E
V O U T L O O K N K E E S P
T O L I G H T P L G A R Y S
```

Bottom	Native	Raft
Chase	Ocean	Resident
Coastal	Oregon	Resourceful
Community	Otter	Romp
Dropping	Outlook	Safety
Group	Pacific	Sink
Hanging	Playful	Speed
Happy	Positive	Vibration
Land	Priority	Water
Light	Quick	

Going Beyond the Beyond

We are part of the animal kingdom, not separate from it. Like all of our planetary brethren, we are born, live, and die. Nobody gets out of here alive. No one lives without loss. In addition to beloved humans, many of us have loved and lost an animal companion. Most find comfort in spiritual beliefs that somehow, somewhere the souls of our dearly departed are close by, looking over us like some sort of guardian angels.

Many animal lovers embrace the concept of the Rainbow Bridge, where our beloved animals greet us after we die and before we move on to whatever is next. The idea of the Rainbow Bridge can be that concept that gets people through the hardest days after the loss of a well-loved furred, scaled, or feathered friend.

Most religious traditions believe that what we humans do in life echoes in eternity. They teach that eternal life is of the soul, not the body. Some religions, including Christianity, Islam, and Judaism, believe in the soul's existence in another afterlife world. Other religions, like many forms of Hinduism and Buddhism, believe in reincarnation. Still others yet, like the spectrum of Pagan belief systems, can include a combination, or even a blending, of afterlife and reincarnation. Whatever the specificity of their beliefs, Americans are strongly spiritual. Ninety two percent believe in God, and 74 percent believe in life after death.*

Humans long for safe passage to the realms beyond earthly life. This cornucopia of possibilities reflects our diversity of belief systems: Heaven, Valhalla, the Summerland, Gan Eden, the Elysian Fields, Jannah, the Great Beyond, Nirvana, Nothingness, the Happy Hunting Ground, Tir Na Nog, the Celestial Kingdoms, Enlightenment, the Otherworld, Vaikuntha, Tian, the Other Side, Peace, or Paradise.

Could the same be true for our animal companions?

Or are our animal companions, based on their capacity for unconditional love, automatically admitted to some sort of animal heaven? Do they wait there for us? Do they exist on many planes, and then pop in when it's our turn to die? Do they somehow find a way to come back as a different animal to take care of us?

No one knows the answers to these questions. There is no scientific proof one way or another. There is quite a controversy around the issue of whether animals have souls. Like all human belief systems, including religion, some say *Yay*, some say *Nay*, and some say *I don't know.*

More than two thirds of us believe in angels. There are plenty of stories of family members communicating with their deceased loved ones from beyond the veil, both animal and human. It could be a strong sense of presence, an overpowering feeling of love, a voice heard on the inside. Many see a continued presence out of the corner of the eye. Some have reported having visions of the breed and approximate time of birth of the next life of their companions, which they have pursued. Some have been miraculously rewarded with the accurate manifestation of that vision, much to their delight at reunion.

According to Lauren, the animals that she has spoken to believe in and have experience of communication after death and even reincarnation. She says:

> When we make a communication connection with an animal, we are connecting with the higher being, not just the physical body that you can see and touch. Many people agree, and animals certainly do, that there exists a duality within all of us. Our physical being that goes about daily life, and the deeper more spiritual side of ourselves sometimes referred to as our soul, or higher consciousness, that lives on after physical death.
>
> I often joke that, when I speak to animals, I do not encounter Jewish cats, Catholic dogs, or even Buddhist llamas. Animals have a spiritual, not religious, perspective and they are firm believers in reincarnation. One wise Malamute named Roo put it this way, "Life is non-ending because life is not limited to the physical bodies you have on earth. There is much more to it." Happily, this means that we are able to connect with the higher being after the death of the body. Generally speaking we can talk to animals who have died until the time that they reincarnate on earth, when they assume new lives, new personalities, and embark on a lifetime filled with new learning opportunities.

This next set of puzzles includes conversations with animal family members who are close to the end or on the Other Side that want to share a message with their beloved humans.

*2015 Pew Forum on Religion and Public Life

Katrina the Cat

Senior cats can experience something like human dementia or Alzheimer's. They may wander around a little dazed and confused and meow constantly. Katrina was an elderly cat on her way to the Other Side. Her family wanted to know how to support her.

Lauren: How do you feel?

Katrina: There is a certain surrender that happens when things become inevitable. We can struggle and do our best and then peace descends. The struggle stops and sweetness replaces it. The final conclusion of death is a reunion of sorts, a return to wholeness. That feeling is always sweet.

Lauren: How will I know when you are ready to go?

Katrina: If I am too weak to move around, or in pain. If you look at me and sense that I am no longer present in my body. Eventually the connection between body and soul is so fine that a breath of wind could wipe it away. Then you must be that breath of wind. But I have no regrets, only beautiful memories. Being next to your heart always made me feel so loved, so secure. As though your heartbeat set the rhythm of my world. Even after I'm gone, I will be with you for a time, and always curled up in your heart. Content, secure, and ever loved.

Animal Wisdom:

___ ___ ___ ___   ___ ___ ___ ___ ___   ___ ___ ___ ___ ___ ___   ___ ___ ___   ___
___ ___ ___ ___ ___ ___   ___ ___ ___ ___ ___   ___ ___ ___   ___ ___ ___ ___
___ ___ ___ ___ ___

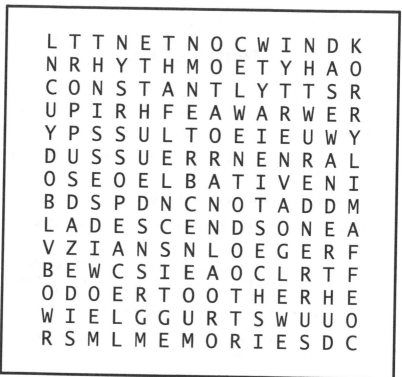

```
L T T N E T N O C W I N D K
N R H Y T H M O E T Y H A O
C O N S T A N T L Y T T S R
U P I R H F E A W A R W E R
Y P S S U L T O E I E U W Y
D U S S U E R R N E N R A L
O S E O E L B A T I V E N I
B D S P D N C N O T A D D M
L A D E S C E N D S O N E A
V Z I A N S N L O E G E R F
B E W C S I E A O C L R T F
O D O E R T O O T H E R H E
W I E L G G U R T S W U U O
R S M L M E M O R I E S D C
```

Body	Inevitable	Soul
Breath	Katrina	Struggle
Conclusion	Memories	Support
Confused	Meow	Surrender
Constantly	Other	Sweetness
Content	Peace	Wander
Curled	Reunion	Wholeness
Dazed	Rhythm	Wind
Descends	Senior	World
Family	Side	

Terry the Dog

Terry was a dog who lived in a Canadian coastal city. She saw beautiful sunsets from her house and she used that experience to reflect on her own end of life.

Lauren: You are an amazing being. You are so bright and full of life. Mischievous too!

Terry: Well, I would never want to be boring.

Lauren: Never. I am doing my best to keep you comfortable, is there anything you need or want?

Terry: No. I'm just enjoying this last bit of time. It's that Golden Time in my life. The sun is setting and there are the final beautiful rays of colors to be enjoyed at the end of the day. Nothing to be done, the day is over, and all that remains is to reflect on the wonder of it all.

Lauren: That's lovely. I have had other animals speak to me about Golden Time, but never so eloquently.

Terry: That's me. Eloquent!

Lauren: And so modest too.

Terry: At this stage, why bother with modesty? And I really want to express what I am feeling to you. It's profound peace and contentment, and satisfaction of a job well done. I'm glad I can share this feeling with you after a lifetime together.

Lauren: Thank you. It has certainly been a beautiful life together.

Animal Wisdom:

— — — — — — — — — — — — — — — —
— — — — — — — — — — — — — — — — —
— — — — — — — — — — — — — — — —

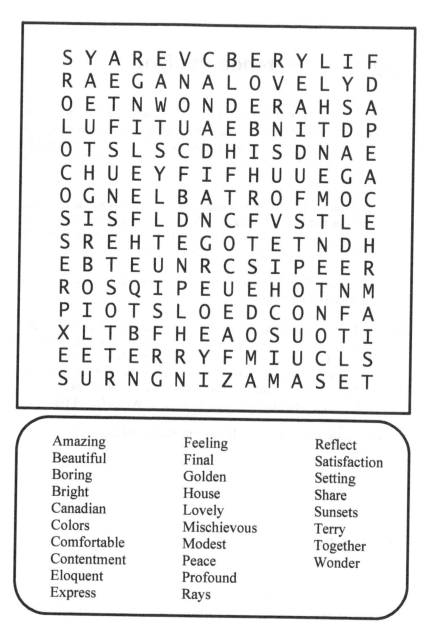

```
S Y A R E V C B E R Y L I F
R A E G A N A L O V E L Y D
O E T N W O N D E R A H S A
L U F I T U A E B N I T D P
O T S L S C D H I S D N A E
C H U E Y F I F H U U E G A
O G N E L B A T R O F M O C
S I S F L D N C F V S T L E
S R E H T E G O T E T N D H
E B T E U N R C S I P E E R
R O S Q I P E U E H O T N M
P I O T S L O E D C O N F A
X L T B F H E A O S U O T I
E E T E R R Y F M I U C L S
S U R N G N I Z A M A S E T
```

Amazing	Feeling	Reflect
Beautiful	Final	Satisfaction
Boring	Golden	Setting
Bright	House	Share
Canadian	Lovely	Sunsets
Colors	Mischievous	Terry
Comfortable	Modest	Together
Contentment	Peace	Wonder
Eloquent	Profound	
Express	Rays	

Patches the Dog

The first dogs were self-domesticated wolves which were attracted to humans at least twelve thousand years ago. Patches was a marvelous small terrier mix who lived on a farm in Quebec. While exploring a heavily wooded area that he knew was not a safe place for him to be, he was killed by a wolf.

Patches: It seems there is a balance between being brave and daring, having fun and being foolhardy. I lived my life to the fullest. I was daring and not limited by my size. And I was very brave, if a little stupid! I learned that bravery and stupidity are distant cousins.

Lauren: I guess life is a learning process right until the end. Do you have anything you want to share?

Patches: I will send to you two things: love in unlimited quantities, and bravery. I will share these things with you in those moments of insecurity. In the times you wake up in emotional darkness, I'll be there for you every time for as long as it takes. I can do more good for you from here. I am grateful for that. Thank you for being such a great friend, nurse, companion, and fellow traveler. We had great times.

Lauren: Thank you. I loved our life together and I always will.

Animal Wisdom:

__ __ __ __ __ __ __   __ __ __ __ __   __ __   __ __ __

__ __ __ __   __ __ __ __ __   __ __   __ __ __ __ __

__ __ __ __ __

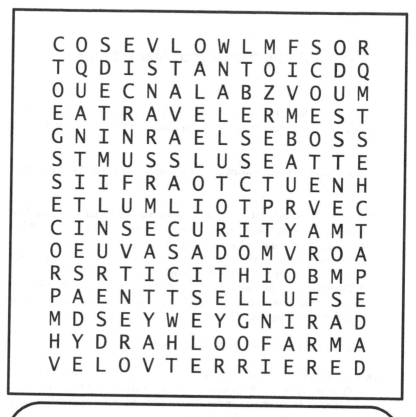

```
C O S E V L O W L M F S O R
T Q D I S T A N T O I C D Q
O U E C N A L A B Z V O U M
E A T R A V E L E R M E S T
G N I N R A E L S E B O S S
S T M U S S L U S E A T T E
S I I F R A O T C T U E N H
E T L U M L I O T P R V E C
C I N S E C U R I T Y A M T
O E U V A S A D O M V R O A
R S R T I C I T H I O B M P
P A E N T T S E L L U F S E
M D S E Y W E Y G N I R A D
H Y D R A H L O O F A R M A
V E L O V T E R R I E R E D
```

Attracted	Heavily	Quebec
Balance	Insecurity	Size
Brave	Learning	Small
Cousins	Love	Stupidity
Daring	Marvelous	Terrier
Distant	Moments	Traveler
Domesticated	Nurse	Unlimited
Farm	Patches	Wolves
Foolhardy	Process	
Fullest	Quantities	

Johnny the Dog of Many Lives

Johnny was a Dachshund in Japan. He showed me images of himself in a past life as a Dutch boy. His Japanese people in this current lifetime were also in the pictures.

Lauren: Thank you for showing me these images. Did we have a previous life together?

Johnny: Yes. My father was a Dutch trader who arranged for me to live with you when he sailed back to Holland for work. You were teaching me, integrating me into Japanese culture. I was like a son to you both. This arrangement went on for many years, until I was an adult and returned to Europe. I could not come to see you, which was very difficult for all of us. Our connection goes beyond the family we have now. We are connected at a soul level, like a spider's web, woven together strong and beautiful.

Lauren: That makes me happy, and sad to lose you.

Johnny: Remember the web connection. It is very old and grows stronger with what we weave from each lifetime. Learn, move forward, grow, and weave. It is very beautiful. Don't feel sad. My death will be the beginning of a new thread in our web.

Animal Wisdom:

___ ___ ___   ___ ___ ___ ___ ___ ___ ___ ___   ___ ___   ___ ___ ___ ___
___ ___ ___ ___ ___ ___ ___ ___ ___   ___ ___ ___ ___   ___ ___
___ ___ ___ ___ ___ ___ ___ ___   ___ ___   ___ ___ ___ ___ ___
___ ___ ___ ___ ___ ___ ___ ___ ___   ___ ___ ___ ___

```
T R W E A V E L B H E S S T
D E E P O R U E E D J T W R
U D T H R E A D R A W R O F
T A E A N U D S P C R O R W
C R O T T T E A C H I N G O
H T F I C O N U R S I G L V
O L F N I E Y F E H M T I E
L U M T S P N E S U A L I N
L D B E G I N N I N G P N K
A A U G S C H Y O D E D P T
N O G R E T O T L C S E H Y
D E R A I U J N M I A L N Y
C U L T U R E W O N M I D E
R T N E M E G N A R R A F U
L W A D Y S R E D I P S F S
```

Adult	Forward	Sailed
Arrangement	Grow	Spider
Beautiful	Happy	Strong
Beginning	Holland	Teaching
Connected	Images	Thread
Culture	Integrated	Trader
Dachshund	Japanese	Weave
Dutch	Johnny	Woven
Europe	Learn	
Family	Pictures	

Snuffi the Rabbit

Snuffi was a very cute, and very opinionated house rabbit living with his family in Tokyo. He says things as he sees them, even after his death.

Snuffi: Well, that was a good long ride, wasn't it? It was all pretty ideal.

Lauren: Glad you think so. I sure did my best for you.

Snuffi: Yeah, I know. And in return, I was cute. So, we both did well. I know you like animals with strong personalities. We are more in your face. We make you laugh and feel things. The sweet animals don't have such an impact on you. Bland. That's how I see it anyway!

Lauren: Hmm. Well, maybe so. I still feel you very much with me, inside of me.

Snuffi: Of course. I'm not that easy to get rid of. The cuteness lingers.

Lauren: And the grumpiness?

Snuffi: You can call it grumpy. I call it discerning. I have refined tastes and could get what I wanted. Why not? You're not so very different.

Lauren: I'm not grumpy.

Snuffi: No, but you are opinionated. There is nothing wrong with being opinionated, as long as you have the right opinions! Want to know the big lesson? Be true to yourself. I always was.

Lauren: And still are.

Snuffi: Yup.

Animal Wisdom:

__ __   _____ __ _____
_____ _____ ____
_____ _____ __
_____ _____ __ __ _____

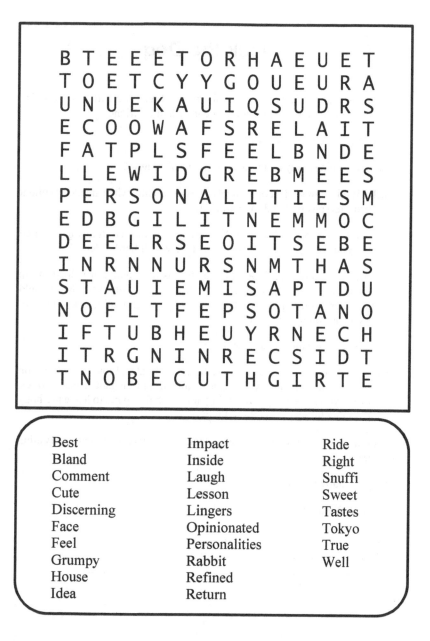

```
B T E E E T O R H A E U E T
T O E T C Y Y G O U E U R A
U N U E K A U I Q S U D R S
E C O O W A F S R E L A I T
F A T P L S F E E L B N D E
L L E W I D G R E B M E E S
P E R S O N A L I T I E S M
E D B G I L I T N E M M O C
D E E L R S E O I T S E B E
I N R N N U R S N M T H A S
S T A U I E M I S A P T D U
N O F L T F E P S O T A N O
I F T U B H E U Y R N E C H
I T R G N I N R E C S I D T
T N O B E C U T H G I R T E
```

Best	Impact	Ride
Bland	Inside	Right
Comment	Laugh	Snuffi
Cute	Lesson	Sweet
Discerning	Lingers	Tastes
Face	Opinionated	Tokyo
Feel	Personalities	True
Grumpy	Rabbit	Well
House	Refined	
Idea	Return	

Jack the Dog

Jack was a delightful German Shepherd who loved life with a passion. He shared some lovely words with his dearest human friend.

Jack: I was elegant, wasn't I?

Lauren: In many ways, but what are you referring to?

Jack: Well, I greeted people nicely. I was around when needed without being too pushy. Kind of charming.

Lauren: Oh yes, very charming. You are greatly missed. It always seemed that you were joyful, and so connected. Was it hard to leave?

Jack: In a way, yes, in a way, no. It was time and you helped me to make a graceful exit, an elegant departure. I'm grateful for that. I could have kept going, powered by love and joy, but really, it would have been hard on me physically.

Lauren: Will we meet again sometime?

Jack: No doubt. We are ideal companions, soulmates. I loved my dance on the earth as Jack and you are a beautiful and elegant dance partner. Thank you for that, for everything, and for helping me to leave my body in a graceful way. I send my love to you.

Lauren: We send you our love, Jack. We miss you and everything about you.

Jack: Goodbye, dear ones.

Animal Wisdom:

— — —   — — — —   — — — — — — — — —
— — — — —   — —   — — — — —   — —
— — — — — — — —   — — —   — — — — — —

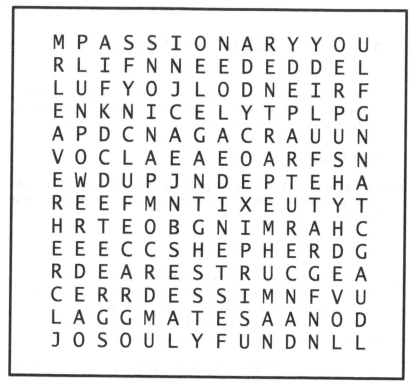

```
M P A S S I O N A R Y Y O U
R L I F N N E E D E D D E L
L U F Y O J L O D N E I R F
E N K N I C E L Y T P L P G
A P D C N A G A C R A U U N
V O C L A E A E O A R F S N
E W D U P J N D E P T E H A
R E E F M N T I X E U T Y T
H R T E O B G N I M R A H C
E E E C C S H E P H E R D G
R D E A R E S T R U C G E A
C E R R D E S S I M N F V U
L A G G M A T E S A A N O D
J O S O U L Y F U N D N L L
```

Charming	Graceful	Missed
Companions	Grateful	Needed
Connected	Greeted	Nicely
Dance	Human	Partner
Dearest	Ideal	Passion
Departure	Jack	Powered
Elegant	Joyful	Pushy
Exit	Leave	Shepherd
Friend	Loved	Soul
German	Mates	

Reinie the Cat

Reinie was a wonderful, sweet street cat adopted by a friend living in Mexico. Her person respected Reinie's repeated requests to be let outside. When she didn't come home for several days, I spoke with her.

Lauren: I am grieving for you.

Reinie: I'm so sorry. You know my path was always to be a street cat, but I was lured, intoxicated, by the love and affection of a family. It was beautiful.

Lauren: Reinie, are you in your body?

Reinie: No. I've moved on. My adventurous nature got the better of me. I strayed too far from home. But I felt comfortable in a way. As though I reaffirmed a connection with the wilder side of life that was such a big part of me. Being out and exploring was the bigger part of my nature. As well as the sweet, and affectionate side.

Lauren: I love you and understand that you had other aspects of your life to explore. What did you learn?

Reinie: I suppose that being true to oneself, one's nature, comes at a cost sometimes. It is always there, sometimes watchful and silent. Sometimes riotous and demanding. Either way, who you are must be heard. To do any less is to waste your life.

Animal Wisdom:

_____ _____ _____ ____

_____ __ _____ __

_____

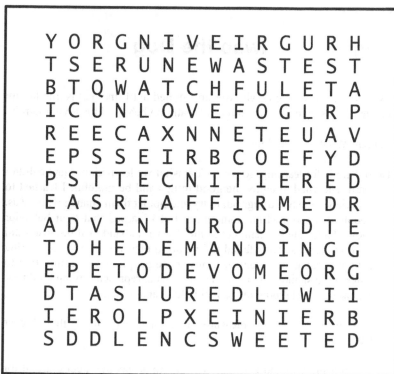

```
Y O R G N I V E I R G U R H
T S E R U N E W A S T E S T
B T Q W A T C H F U L E T A
I C U N L O V E F O G L R P
R E E C A X N N E T E U A V
E P S S E I R B C O E F Y D
P S T T E C N I T I E R E D
E A S R E A F F I R M E D R
A D V E N T U R O U S D T E
T O H E D E M A N D I N G G
E P E T O D E V O M E O R G
D T A S L U R E D L I W I I
I E R O L P X E I N I E R B
S D D L E N C S W E E T E D
```

Adopted	Love	Silent
Adventurous	Lured	Strayed
Affection	Moved	Street
Aspects	Path	Sweet
Bigger	Reaffirmed	Waste
Demanding	Reinie	Watchful
Explore	Repeated	Wilder
Grieving	Requests	Wonderful
Heard	Riotous	
Intoxicated	Side	

Iwao the Dog

Iwao was a Japanese dog who was abandoned until finding his true family late in life. I spoke with him after his death, on behalf of his loving family.

Lauren: What are you doing?

Iwao: Life is for learning, so we review what we learned, or maybe didn't learn. I learned to enjoy the good things and be grateful. I learned to experience the bad things but to try and not let them change who I was. People disappointed me sometimes, but I learned that their behavior showed a failing in them, not in me. I wasn't abandoned because I did anything wrong. They failed to live up to their promise to me. Caring for me became inconvenient. I pity those people whose connection to others is so shallow. You, on the other hand, represent loving kindness. Thank you for helping me to feel valued and loved.

Lauren: It was truly my pleasure. You gave back more than I ever gave you.

Iwao: I felt grateful and I want to say that to all people. Feel grateful for all you have. Don't wait until it is taken away to miss it. Whether it is your health, friends, family, anything. Don't wait until it is gone to appreciate it. Be grateful today and every day. That is my message to you.

Animal Wisdom:

_____ ____ _____ __
____ ____ _____
_____ _____
_____ ____

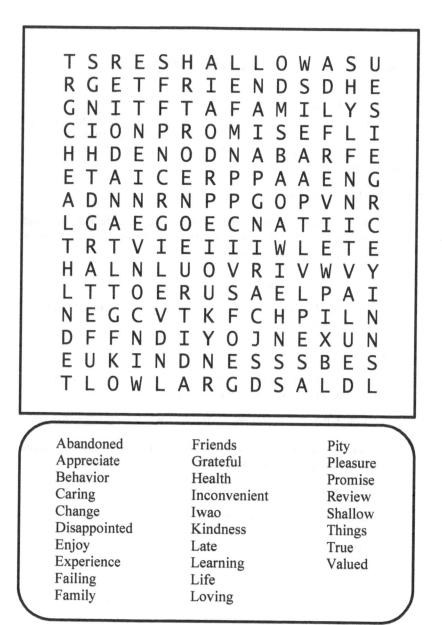

```
T S R E S H A L L O W A S U
R G E T F R I E N D S D H E
G N I T F T A F A M I L Y S
C I O N P R O M I S E F L I
H H D E N O D N A B A R F E
E T A I C E R P P A A E N G
A D N N R N P P G O P V N R
L G A E G O E C N A T I I C
T R T V I E I I W L E T E
H A L N L U O V R I V W V Y
L T T O E R U S A E L P A I
N E G C V T K F C H P I L N
D F F N D I Y O J N E X U N
E U K I N D N E S S S B E S
T L O W L A R G D S A L D L
```

Abandoned	Friends	Pity
Appreciate	Grateful	Pleasure
Behavior	Health	Promise
Caring	Inconvenient	Review
Change	Iwao	Shallow
Disappointed	Kindness	Things
Enjoy	Late	True
Experience	Learning	Valued
Failing	Life	
Family	Loving	

Kobi the Dog

The human-dog bond stretches back millennia. Interestingly, ancient Egyptians revered their dogs. When a family dog died, the owners shaved off their eyebrows, smeared mud in their hair, and mourned aloud for days. Kobi was a wonderful and wise German Shepherd. He shared these thoughts shortly after his death.

Lauren: Hi Kobi. We miss you so much.

Kobi: Oh, I know, I feel your pain. I wish you could feel the joy and happiness I feel. The total love, the light, the freedom. My only grief at passing is that you and dad are in pain.

Lauren: You have left a big hole that we simply cannot fill.

Kobi: Odd, since I am much bigger, brighter, and stronger now than I ever was. How hard that I cannot share this with those I love.

Lauren: Will you be near us for a while?

Kobi: Yes, I will be very near for a few days. Then I will be accessible to you in your quiet times and when you call me.

Lauren: Good, thank you. Is there anything else you want to say to us?

Kobi: I love you and always will. I will be with dad when he walks on the beach. It was special to me and to him.

Lauren: Yes, thank you.

Kobi: Thank you for your love and all your gifts.

Animal Wisdom:

__ __ __ __   __ __   __ __   __ __ __ __ __ __ __ __ __
__ __ __ __ __ __ __ __ __ __   __ __ __ __
__ __ __ __ __   __ __   __ __ __ __   __ __ __ __ __
__ __ __ __ __

```
L O V S N A I T P Y G E E I
T D U O L A I N E L L I M S
H T A N E N E R G B O N D E
G I F T S S E N I P P A H T
I M I E G N I S S A P A I N
L E C C Y S S P E C I A L O
O S D H R E T H G I R B D N
V N E E C R B R B M C D E T
E I V C I A O R O I E N R T
H A A A T L E D O N G I E V
E S H O L E E B R W G G V O
N E S V T E I U Q E S E E N
A F T E R K O B I N E A R R
R D E F S M E A R E D A T H
```

Accessible	Hair	Passing
Aloud	Happiness	Quiet
Beach	Hole	Revered
Bigger	Kobi	Shaved
Bond	Light	Smeared
Brighter	Love	Special
Egyptians	Millenia	Stronger
Eyebrows	Mourned	Times
Freedom	Near	
Gifts	Pain	

Roo the Dog

Roo was a delightful Malamute who led me down the path of working with animals. This breed accompanied Siberian Mahlemut nomads across the Bering Straits into what is now known as Alaska.

Lauren: Is there something that fundamentally connects all of us on earth?

Roo: Yes, very much so. Despite our differences, we all eat, sleep, take care of our young, and dream our dreams.

Lauren: Can you share one of your dreams?

Roo: I dream of a time when people and animals are treated with the respect they deserve. When each being is regarded as an individual with their own rights and feelings, then the earth will be in a good place. This fundamental lack of understanding not just between people and animals, but between species and races, means that we often disregard each other's needs and wants. When you truly understand someone, then you make choices that can benefit all. The lack of tolerance and understanding are the main problems.

Lauren: How can truly understanding someone help those who have loved and lost?

Roo: We are all connected. Whether you know or feel it or not, it is there. Learning to make a connection with who a being really is, lights up that pathway between you. It helps you to feel each other more strongly.

Animal Wisdom:

— — — — — — — — — — — — — —
— — — — — — — — — —   — — — — — —
— — — — — — — — — —   — — — — — — —
— — — — — —

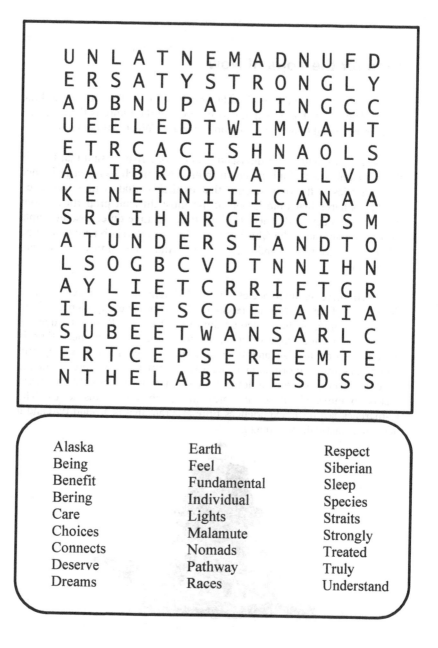

```
U N L A T N E M A D N U F D
E R S A T Y S T R O N G L Y
A D B N U P A D U I N G C C
U E E L E D T W I M V A H T
E T R C A C I S H N A O L S
A A I B R O O V A T I L V D
K E N E T N I I I C A N A A
S R G I H N R G E D C P S M
A T U N D E R S T A N D T O
L S O G B C V D T N N I H N
A Y L I E T C R R I F T G R
I L S E F S C O E E A N I A
S U B E E T W A N S A R L C
E R T C E P S E R E E M T E
N T H E L A B R T E S D S S
```

Alaska	Earth	Respect
Being	Feel	Siberian
Benefit	Fundamental	Sleep
Bering	Individual	Species
Care	Lights	Straits
Choices	Malamute	Strongly
Connects	Nomads	Treated
Deserve	Pathway	Truly
Dreams	Races	Understand

Time for the Yoga of Now

Now is the only time that is simultaneously the past, the present, and the future. The past is the now that was before and the future is the now that is yet to be. Mind boggling to consider, isn't it? What is time, really?

Nearly two and a half thousand years ago, Aristotle said that time is the most unknown of all unknown things. Not much has changed since then. Physics is the only science that explicitly studies time, but even physicists agree that time is one of the most difficult properties of our universe to understand. There is clock time, relative time, absolute time, the linear continuum, the wheel of time, time travel, relativistic time, time dilation, space-time, and tea time. And the times, they are a changing.

Then there is interspecies time. Different animals perceive time differently. Time perception refers to the subjective experience of the passage of time, or the perceived duration of events. Research suggests that across a wide range of species, the way each experiences time is directly related to size and how rapidly an animal's nervous system processes sensory information. Generally, the smaller a creature is, and the faster its metabolic rate, the slower time seems to pass. For a fly, the world seems to move about seven times slower than it seems to us. The leatherback sea turtle experiences time at a rate that is around two and a half times faster than a human.

Flies avoid being swatted because they are able to perceive time much more slowly than we do. To us it looks like slow motion. While clock time is really passing at the same speed, the fly's eyes send updates to its brain far more frequently than a human's eyes, and its mental processes are similarly much more rapid than ours. Have you ever experienced the time slow down effect, where everything takes forever and there are moments between the moments? It often happens during a crisis of some kind. It's unforgettable.

Although physical clock time appears to be more or less objective, psychological time is subjective and potentially malleable. Time flies when you are having fun and a watched pot never boils. Sometimes we have no time, and sometimes we have too much time on our hands. And that can change in an instant.

There are so many ways to explore and experience time, from precise tick tock schedules and alarms, to the shifting times of sunrise and sunset, the cycle of the seasons, and internal personal rhythms. Is there time enough for love? Time is at once precise, relative, and an illusion.

> Time isn't precious at all, because it is an illusion. What you perceive as precious is not time but the one point that is out of time: the Now. That is precious indeed. The more you are focused on time—past and future—the more you miss the Now, the most precious thing there is.
>
> —Eckhart Tolle

Our brains take us out of the now. They can hinder us from fully experiencing the sublime preciousness of an exquisite moment by thinking about our to-do lists while watching a sunset. Texting someone while driving also takes us out of the now and could be life threatening to others as well as ourselves. Our fast-paced, technologically multitasking society tries to trick us into not being here in the now. But we can overcome this challenge with some help from our friends.

Animals live in the now. They help bring us to the present moment. In our daily lives, our interspecies companions help us get out of our heads and into our hearts and bodies. There is a deeply personal yoga of sharing a life with an animal family member. *Yoga* means union and brings us back to now. It establishes and cultivates a harmonious connection between our inner worlds and outer worlds. Maybe that's why so many hatha yoga poses (asanas) are named after animals.

The asana menagerie includes mammals like dog, cat, cow, camel, horse, lion, monkey, and bull. Bird poses include eagle, peacock, partridge, swan, crane, rooster, pigeon, and heron. Asanas are even named after and invoke frogs and fishes, cobras, crocodiles, and turtles. The insect kingdom is represented by locust, scorpion, and firefly. It can be a real stretching safari.

Other forms of yoga bring us to the now as well. We know that hatha yoga stretches our bodies and makes them more flexible. Mantra can help quiet the mind. Pranayama can help us focus on breath. And doing a puzzle, a form of Dharana yoga, can bring our minds fully into the present.

Wise people, since the dawn of recorded history, from ancient Egyptian mathematicians to King Solomon to Benjamin Franklin, practiced the yoga of puzzles to keep their minds supple by bringing them into the present moment.

Puzzles come in all different forms. Whether visual, language, mathematical, physical, logical, metaphysical, or mechanical, each puzzle tests and expands our varied intelligences in one way or another. We solve these mysteries with whatever clues and skills we have.

This yoga for the brain also expands our intuition and helps us develop a sort of puzzle vision super power. It takes us beyond thinking. This super power is a fairy godmother revealing a genius X factor that shows us the way through that we have not conceived before. A novel approach pops into our heads. Images rise up into our mind's eye. Is it clairvoyance? Guidance? Expanded intuition? Inspiration? Regardless of the label, the sense is that of absolute knowingness.

We experience the perfect harmony of the universe; the solution comes, like magic.

And it comes only when we are fully present.

Right here. Right now.

Now is a great time. Enjoy it!

Elephant

This female elephant in Botswana is the head of a small family.

Elephant: What do you see when you look at us?

Lauren: Beauty, grace, motherhood, wisdom. What do you see when you look at humans?

Elephant: This is gradually changing over time.

Lauren: I assume that is because there is no more hunting here.

Elephant: Yes. Slowly the stories we tell our children are changing. We do not fully trust people, but eventually, gradually, our trust is growing.

Lauren: How can you tell the difference between people?

Elephant: First we watch, then we feel. If you move slowly and keep your distance, that is a good sign. Elephants communicate through vibration across distances. Through the earth, and through the water too.

Lauren: You sense physical vibration. Do you use vibrations like telepathy or intuition too?

Elephant: Yes, sometimes we do.

Lauren: And the vibration you feel from humans, is that different than from elephants?

Elephant: Yes, I suppose so. That nonphysical vibration is what we use to talk to each other and it includes feelings, and I suppose you would say intention.

Lauren: Can you make mistakes in reading people?

Elephant: Sometimes, but not often. Intention is very clear.

Animal Wisdom:

__ __ __ __ __ __ __ __ __   __ __ __ __ __ __ __ __
__ __ __ __   __ __ __ __ __ __ __   __ __ __
__ __ __ __ __ __   __ __ __ __ __ __   __ __ __ __
__ __ __ __ __

```
I N T E N O I T A R B I V A
D N B T L D I S T A N C E D
I R O E L A M E F T N N O M
R A E T A C I N U M M O C I
D F G H I U N I A T H N E R
S G N I H C T A W R E P F I
R O I M Y I E Y E R W H W N
I T D A O H N H D G I Y H G
I K A N E N T L A R S S N N
C L E A R O I A D A D I S I
P A R W M H O E P C O C A W
K T E S C S N L O E M A U O
H D T T R U S T E R L L T R
H A A O T N A H P E L E N G
W O W B R D S S E I R O T S
```

Admiring	Feel	Reading
Beauty	Female	Stories
Botswana	Grace	Talk
Children	Growing	Telepathy
Clear	Herd	Trust
Communicate	Intention	Vibration
Distance	Intuition	Watching
Earth	Motherhood	Water
Elephant	Nonphysical	Wisdom

Japanese Giant Salamander

Since ancient times, Japanese Giant Salamanders have been known as the Hanzaki. They live in and around rivers in Japan. Growing up to five feet long, their biology has changed little in millions of years and has earned them the title of *living dinosaurs*. They smell like pepper, are astonishingly quick, and make noises that sound a bit like a child. With a keen sense of smell and special receptors on their skin that sense vibrations in the water, as well as absorb oxygen, these mysterious nocturnal beings have successfully adapted over millennia. Now their species is critically threatened. This wise soul lives in a zoo in Tokyo.

Salamander: I am one of the last of an ancient species. Look at me closely, you may not see me much longer.

Lauren: What do you want people to know about you?

Salamander: When we lose species, the vibration of the earth changes and can never be reclaimed. Everything is a vibration and we all, in the natural world, create a harmony. It is the song of Mother Earth. Humans are destroying so much; so many natural voices are silenced. I do not know what this world will look like soon. But there will be places of silence where species with wisdom once lived. Look and listen now. Time is running out.

Animal Wisdom:

— — — — — — — — — — —

— — — — — — — — — — — — — — — —

— — — — — — — — — — — — — — — —

— — — — — — — — — — — — —

```
P R I V E R S R E S G G B E
R R H A R M O N Y M W N R V
E A R T H Y E T O O H I O E
P N E E K S S T R I Y V S S
P M P C C T H L H O L I B L
E N H N R E D N A M A L A S
P Y A E R R P Y A D O I I F
W I N L S I G T I T C D A M
O M Z I T O H N O E U D A T
I N A S L U O C P R A R L U
D E K O L S Q S S P S A A T
L L I L A N R U T C O N N L
E B E U A T N E I C N A R T
H M R W I S D O M C I L Y B
S S E C I O V E I G K N G S
```

Absorb	Living	Salamander
Adapted	Millions	Silence
Ancient	Mother	Smell
Biology	Mysterious	Song
Dinosaurs	Natural	Special
Earth	Nocturnal	Voices
Giant	Pepper	Wisdom
Hanzaki	Quick	World
Harmony	Receptors	
Keen	Rivers	

53 American Black Bear

In many Native American cultures, bears represent introspection, inner attunement, and integration. Bear medicine has the healing power to restore harmony and balance through the great sleep of hibernation. All of bear's energy goes to turning inward in the safety of a cave. Bears can go up to seven and a half months without eating, drinking, or eliminating during this time of sacred pause. Its body recycles waste into protein, a mystery that science has yet to solve. This majestic being talks about the cyclical nature of introspection.

Lauren: What can you tell me about introspection from a bear's point of view?

Bear: There is a lot happening in the world, and in life. So much of what it all means is how you interpret it. If you don't take the time to digest things, to internalize them, then so many of life's experiences pass you by. It's a bit like how we bears operate with food. There is a period of great activity, a time to gather food. Then we feast, in other words, we take it all in. Then we digest or interpret. Make whatever we have taken in a part of us. In this way, we gather nutrition or wisdom from what we have taken in. Then we rest. This is the rhythm of the bear.

Animal Wisdom:

___ _____ __

_____ _____

__ _____ __ _____

_____

```
T H E Z I L A N R E T N I E R
H Y N T N H M C O F O A I N T
R O O S T E R B T I P M E T M
E C I R R N E L T I T E E E H
S H T A O E P A N I V R D O T
U N I E S R R C E B P I R I Y
A H R B P G E K M R C C T N H
P E T G E Y S S E I S A U Y R
S A U T C R E T N M A N E Y E
D L N S T C N E U O C E C N N
P I T E I I T A T D R H N O N
S N O G O L C I T S E J A M I
F G G I N C A R A I D E L R A
F O O D T Y V R E W O P A A I
N S I G H C E V I T A N B H T
```

Activity	Food	Medicine
American	Harmony	Native
Attunement	Healing	Nutrition
Balance	Hibernation	Pause
Bear	Inner	Power
Black	Integration	Represent
Cave	Internalize	Rhythm
Cyclic	Interpret	Sacred
Digest	Introspection	Wisdom
Energy	Majestic	

Chimpanzee

Chimpanzees and humans have 97 percent of their DNA in common. Recent genetic comparisons suggest that chimps have actually evolved more since the two species parted from a common ancestor about five million years ago, bringing them currently into their evolutionary Stone Age. Chimps have been using stone tools in Africa for at least 4300 years. Some groups use stones as hammers and anvils to crack open nuts. Others use twigs to fish for termites. Some make spears for hunting. I asked this chimp what he thinks about evolution.

Lauren: What do you think about being a chimpanzee?

Chimp: We are smart and proud and very much like you.

Lauren: Yes, I was wondering about chimps and what you think about evolution.

Chimp: Soul or body evolution?

Lauren: Both.

Chimp: Well the body evolves, I guess, and adapts to changes through time. I think body evolution happens without much of our conscious thought. Though I guess we make some choices, like using tools and so on, that might impact evolution over the long-term. The soul evolves in a space where there is no time. I believe, in the timeless space, evolution can happen faster, and perhaps also that you as an individual have a more active role to play.

Animal Wisdom:

—— ——— ——————————
————— —— ———— ————
——— —————— —— ———
—————

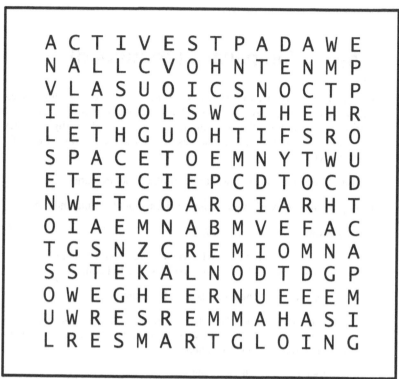

```
A C T I V E S T P A D A W E
N A L L C V O H N T E N M P
V L A S U O I C S N O C T P
I E T O O L S W C I H E H R
L E T H G U O H T I F S R O
S P A C E T O E M N Y T W U
E T E I C I E P C D T O C D
N W F T C O A R O I A R H T
O I A E M N A B M V E F A C
T G S N Z C R E M I O M N A
S S T E K A L N O D T D G P
O W E G H E E R N U E E E M
U W R E S R E M M A H A S I
L R E S M A R T G L O I N G
```

Active	Crack	Soul
Adapts	Evolution	Space
Ancestor	Faster	Stones
Anvils	Fish	Termites
Body	Genetic	Thought
Changes	Hammers	Timeless
Chimpanzee	Impact	Tools
Choices	Individual	Twigs
Common	Proud	
Conscious	Smart	

55 Chimpanzee (continued)

Chimpanzees have been observed watching sunsets, doing rain dances, and throwing rocks at specific trees. These rituals around nature imply a spiritual instinct in our closest evolutionary relatives, which suggests they have souls, or some form of consciousness. I asked our chimp friend for his perspective.

Lauren: Tell me more about what you think of soul evolution.

Chimp: In the soul, we have so many choices about learning and changing.

Lauren: How do we have choices?

Chimp: We have choices as to what bodies we choose to come into, and the situations in which we find ourselves able to learn.

Lauren: Like you being here in this zoo, for example.

Chimp: Sure. Physically it's not very interesting, but the lack of a physically active life does move you inward. Most certainly I have more time to reflect on things here.

Lauren: What have you discovered?

Chimp: I see many types of people, and their emotions. I see the same sort of types in chimps. Some are selfish, some generous. Nurturing, or not. It does make me think that we are all learning the same sorts of lessons, just in different bodies.

Lauren: Brilliant, I agree with you. Thank you very much and I'm so happy to be able to learn from you today.

Chimp: Wonderful.

Animal Wisdom:

—— —— —— —— ——   —— —— ——   —— —— —— ——   —— ——   —— —— ——

—— —— —— ——   —— —— —— —— ——   —— —— —— ——   —— —— ——

```
S G N I W O R H T L T H E A
N S S E I D O B A D R G L R
O T E E A N S U O R E N E G
S D S N V O T U L A E I A W
S E A R S I E M O W S H R I
E G N I R U T R U N R C N N
L E A I L D O A O I I T I S
F K P E A B R I L L I A N T
I S U N S E T S C E R W G I
S T C K F A O H A S R N N N
H E C L U U G N I G N A H C
S O E T L U F R E D N O W T
R C I O O B S E R V E D C T
T S N O I T O M E I M P L Y
```

Bodies	Inward	Selfish
Brilliant	Learning	Situations
Changing	Lessons	Soul
Consciousness	Nurturing	Spiritual
Dances	Observed	Sunsets
Emotions	Rain	Throwing
Generous	Reflect	Trees
Imply	Relatives	Watching
Instinct	Rocks	Wonderful

Ivan the Raven

Ivan is a raven who lives in southern California. He has a deep connection with the heritage of his species.

Lauren: What can you tell me about ravens as a species?

Ivan: We represent many things to many cultures.

Lauren: Yes. Some good, some perhaps not so good.

Ivan: Which is true of anyone, is it not? The shadow side, and the light side. We have different missions and objectives depending on where in the world we live, what culture we are in. Here we help tie the land to the people. Mostly the old ways are gone now, though some remain true to the ancient knowledge and the interplay between people and nature. We ravens are in between the ancient world of power, magic, life, creation, and death. When people journey into that in-between space (which includes meditation, magic, and other rituals), we are there as guides. Sometimes hosts, sometimes messengers between the unconscious mind of the human, and the day-to-day conscious mind. The unconscious mind is a doorway to the soul, the higher realms. It is not an end or a destination of itself, though people treat it that way. It is a portal through which we can travel to the deeper places within the soul, or between the worlds.

Animal Wisdom:

_____ _____ _____ __ _
_____ __ _____ ___
_____

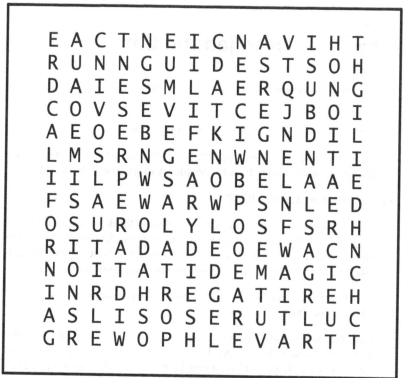

```
E A C T N E I C N A V I H T
R U N N G U I D E S T S O H
D A I E S M L A E R Q U N G
C O V S E V I T C E J B O I
A E O E B E F K I G N D I L
L M S R N G E N W N E N T I
I I L P W S A O B E L A A E
F S A E W A R W P S N L E D
O S U R O L Y L O S F S R H
R I T A D A D E O E W A C N
N O I T A T I D E M A G I C
I N R D H R E G A T I R E H
A S L I S O S E R U T L U C
G R E W O P H L E V A R T T
```

Ancient	Knowledge	Power
California	Land	Raven
Creation	Life	Realms
Cultures	Light	Represent
Deep	Magic	Rituals
Doorway	Meditation	Shadow
Guides	Messengers	Travel
Heritage	Missions	World
Hosts	Objectives	
Ivan	Portal	

Kadijah the Cat

Kadijah is a wonderfully insightful being who spoke to me about cat consciousness.

Lauren: Why do people find cats to be so mysterious?

Kadijah: Because we have our own priorities, many of which are unknown, or not understood by people. And we like it that way!

Lauren: What are cat priorities?

Kadijah: It varies from cat to cat. But why do you think we sleep so much? Do you really think that we are idle? Snoozing our life away? No. Sleep time is a time when we sleep, yes. But it is also a time when the mind disengages and we can easily enter into another consciousness.

Lauren: Is this the kind of consciousness that we have when we die and return home, back to Source?

Kadijah: No, this is more of an in-between level. It is the realm where the body and the soul intertwine. Where creativity, greater purpose, and ideas can take shape, and then can be made manifest in the physical. The body is such a low vibration. Our soul, our higher consciousness, is a much higher vibration. To access information there, to function on that level, we must leave the body consciousness. Sleep is an easy way to do that.

Lauren: Sometimes people do that through meditation.

Kadijah: Yes, and certain animals do that too.

Animal Wisdom:

— — — — — — — — — — — —
— — — — — — — — — — — — — — —
— — — — — — — — — — — — — — — —
— — — — — —

```
B L O U U N D E R S T O O D R
D E R E A A C C E S S L E E P
M V I S L A C I S Y H P S A N
E E D N O I T C N U F S H N I
S L K S G I M S M I E H I E N
O D A U R D I S E N G A G E S
P I D O E D N I S F T P H W I
R A I I T I D U O O I E E T G
U R J R N R O S A R D N R E H
P R A E E I E H O M E A A B T
G A H T C T E W A A A Y T M F
O A U S Y T I V I T A E R C U
H R N Y S N O O Z I N G I G L
N O H M E R V N W O N K N U I
C I N T E R T W I N E S I O N
```

Access	Idle	Priorities
Being	Information	Purpose
Between	Insightful	Return
Consciousness	Intertwine	Shape
Creativity	Kadijah	Sleep
Disengages	Level	Snoozing
Function	Manifest	Understood
Higher	Mind	Unknown
Home	Mysterious	
Idea	Physical	

Great Horned Owl

Owls are thought by many to be wise, but do owls think of themselves so? This great horned owl in western Oregon expresses her views.

Lauren: Many of the world's cultures think that owls are wise. Is it true?

Owl: Of course! Much of it has to do with our perspective, our patience, and our powers of observation.

Lauren: Please tell me more about that.

Owl: Perspective, because we fly above everything and have eyes that see well in both day and night. The world is laid bare during the day and shrouded at night. But so many creatures come out at night. The energy is very different. It is quieter, and more open to possibilities. We are patient. We wait. We wait for the perfect mate. We wait for our prey. We watch, oh so carefully. We are a bridge between the daylight and the nighttime worlds, we thrive in both.

Lauren: What is wisdom to you?

Owl: We attempt to pass our wisdom down through the generations. We are keepers of wisdom and teachers of what we learn. Knowing about things is one thing, understanding them is another. Many seek to know; only the wise strive to understand.

Animal Wisdom:

___ ___ __ _____ __

_____ _____

____ ____ _____

```
N I G H T T I M E T A M T S
H O R N E D H E H C T A W H
G N I W O N K R K E Y S P R
T R O T H G I L Y A D E W O
I P E E A V S C D O R R M U
I O P A E V S A D S E U E D
P W A C T L R R P Y U T N E
D E T H U N D E R S T A N D
E R I E R S C F S T K E E S
A S E R U T L U C B R R V W
N D N S I S I L N G O C O E
G W C V H A E L Y T Y O B I
K E E P E R S Y W I S E A V
U K N Q U I E T E R A B O W
```

Above	Horned	Quieter
Bare	Keepers	Seek
Carefully	Knowing	Shrouded
Creatures	Mate	Teachers
Cultures	Nighttime	Thrive
Daylight	Observation	Understand
Energy	Patience	Views
Eyes	Perspective	Watch
Great	Powers	Wise

Wild Horse

Horses are one of humans' greatest companions. Our domesticated partnership has been going for around six thousand years. There still are many wild horses in the western United States. This particular horse lives in Utah. He speaks on behalf of his species.

Lauren: How do horses see themselves as a species?

Wild horse: We see ourselves as walkers of the land, and as a bridge between humans and Mother Earth. Because of the way that we graze the grass, and walk on the crust of the earth, we are very grounded, very connected to the planet. Humans, most humans, are not as grounded, not as connected. They have lost feeling with the earth.

Lauren: And horses help humans to reconnect?

Wild horse: Yes, that is correct. We help to heal the separation that humans experience when their lives are too full and their minds must focus on too many things. We are created from a union of earth and sky and if you look deep into my eyes, you will see the land and the stars reflected within.

Lauren: That is beautiful, as are you.

Wild horse: Thank you. We are a very proud species, and very honored to serve Mother Earth in this way.

Animal Wisdom:

— — — —　— — — —　— — — —　— — —

— — — —　— —　— — — — — —　— — —

— — — — — — —　— —　— — —　— — — —

— — — — — —

```
L O E A R T H D O G R A Z E
K W I L D S D O E R H E A L
E P I N E E P M L A N D T L
O T P A R T N E R S H I P U
H E E W O A O S C S U C O F
E V Y A N E I T E I O T S O
F R O L O R N I T M E H A E
R E T K H G U C P S A S N H
D S S E P A R A T I O N C O
S N U R N E N T E N A L P C
R T R S O I T E G D I R B O
A T C H O H E D U O R P S O
T C E N N O C E R U L W I T
S H S I L U F I T U A E B N
```

Beautiful	Graze	Reconnect
Bridge	Greatest	Separation
Companions	Heal	Serve
Crust	Honored	Species
Domesticated	Horse	Stars
Earth	Land	Union
Focus	Partnership	Utah
Full	Planet	Walkers
Grass	Proud	Wild

Sugar the Dog

Sugar is a Labrador living in Taiwan with his family. His main person is a dog trainer. Sugar reflects on the importance of empathy and understanding between people and dogs.

Lauren: We have learned a lot from each other.

Sugar: We are both teachers and we are both students. When you realized that honoring the individual, whether animal or human, was essential, then the real learning began. It's not about dog training. Dog training is just behavior. How a dog behaves reflects their inner being and how they see themselves and their relationships with the world and their people. You have many tools to work with dogs now. But the biggest tool you have is understanding, and respect. Once the connection is made on that level, then the other tools will be more effective. Without the respectful connection with the individual dog, your tools are worthless. Remember that dogs are not machines.

Lauren: Good advice, thank you. What do you enjoy most in your life?

Sugar: For a dog, running free is always the most fun. But I don't believe we can fully feel free in our body unless we also feel free in our hearts.

Lauren: That sounds right. And how do we feel free in our hearts?

Sugar: Love, of course. Love is what makes your heart fly. Bodies run, but hearts fly free.

Animal Wisdom:

_ _ _ _ _   _ _ _ _ _   _ _ _ _ _ _   _ _ _ _ _ _
_ _   _ _ _ _ _ _ _ _ _ _ _   _ _ _ _ _

```
G F I V E M A C H I N E S S
A Y R E S P E C T O O P U L
N R H E R E N N I E I E S O
I S T C E L F E R H T O T O
M T A W H A G Y S R C P U T
A R T O C U W N O I E L D R
L A B R A D O R I J N E E A
N I G L E I L E A R N I N G
S N B D T V Y E M M O E T U
B E H A V I O R B P C N S S
R R L A A D V I C E A C O I
N E S S E N T I A L G T L H
R R U N N I N G N A M U H O
T A I W A N V E F A M I L Y
```

Advice	Human	Running
Animal	Individual	Students
Behavior	Inner	Sugar
Connection	Labrador	Taiwan
Empathy	Learning	Teachers
Enjoy	Machines	Tools
Essential	People	Trainer
Family	Reflects	World
Free	Relationships	
Honoring	Respect	

End Game

Spending this time together with our animal planet mates, we are reminded that we are all family. Different branches of the same tree. Though we have sometimes radically different anatomy and physiology, our individual hearts beat, we breathe, eat, sleep, eliminate, and procreate. We each eventually die, the substance of our bodies returning to the earth as our spirit goes to whatever comes after physical death. Heart and soul, are we more alike than not? You decide.

Every being on this beautiful and majestic planet has its place in the web of life. Each is on their own path. The vibrations of earth are changing fast. All creatures, great and small, agree on that. When we remember to notice the beauty around us our hearts set a loving beat for the world. Being who we are, individually and collectively, creates beauty inside and out.

We call on the qualities of other species to make us better people. Animals permeate our consciousness and are with us all the time, whether we live with an animal family member or not. Animals are good medicine for humans. The sight of a hummingbird brings joy. When we see a snake, it can remind us that we might need to shed an old skin, or to pay attention to dangers lurking close by.

We can become interspecies communicators with practice, persistence, and patience. We have the ability to share a private, deeply personal language with other species on our earth. Many of us see symbols in the animals we run across in our daily lives. From dragonflies to butterflies to ravens to larger critters, when we see these, we are touched with joy and wonder. We are reminded of the freedom of flight, and the preciousness of wild things, even in the midst of our cities.

Direct communication with other animals deepens our appreciation for the intelligence, magic, and mystery of all beings, whether they're of the air, water, or land. Animals have preferences, perspectives, and opinions. We understand that we never know what we will see through another set of eyes until we look.

Animals help remind us to remember how important it is to express love in everything we do. The richness of our connections transcends color and clothes. Our lives are enriched and enhanced by our friendships. And we remember to take quiet time too. Silence reveals and nurtures the extraordinary inner you.

Our animal planet mates remind us to be true to ourselves.

That everyone wants to be loved and wanted.

That you get out of life what you put into it.

To be grateful today and every day.

That the present is a gift. Be here now to enjoy it.

Connection is a joy.

Love is the answer.

Wisdom comes in many forms.

And to live and let live.

Answers

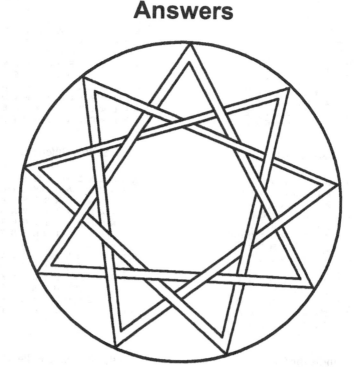

We need another and a wiser and perhaps a more mystical concept of animals. We patronize them for their incompleteness, for their tragic fate of having taken form so far below ourselves.... And therein we err, and greatly err. For the animal shall not be measured by man. In a world older and more complete than ours they moved finished and complete, gifted with extensions of the senses we have lost or never attained, living by voices we shall never hear. They are not brethren, they are not underlings; they are other nations, caught with ourselves in the net of life and time, fellow prisoners of the splendour and travail of the earth.
—*Henry Beston,* The Outermost House, *1928*

1. Aslan the Cat

2. Allie the Dog

3. Barred Owl

4. Saddle-Billed Stork

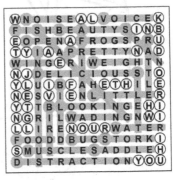

5. Indie the Cat

6. Lilac-Breasted Roller Bird

7. Giraffe

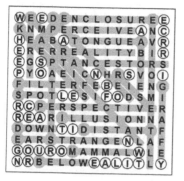

8. Fish Eagle

9. Cape Buffalo

10. Hippopotamus

11. Baby Elephant

12. Malachite Kingfisher

13. Deer

14. Hippos

15. Waterbuck

16. Desert Tortoise

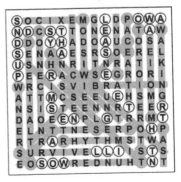

17. Mongoose

18. Baboon Mother

19. Muskoka the Horse

20. Simon the Cat

21. Mongoose Mother

22. Meredith the Bunny

23. Young Buck

24. Orejas the Cat

25. Carpenter Ant

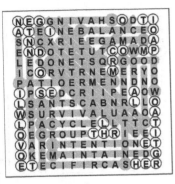

26. Contented Cow

27. Octopus

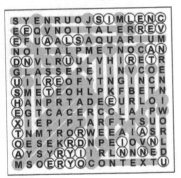

28. Oso the Dog

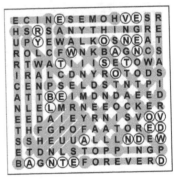

29. Sanctuary Elephant

30. Sanctuary Elephant (continued)

31. Bella the Dog

32. Bella the Dog (continued)

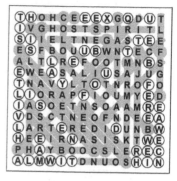

33. Gemsbok Antelope

34. Kenji the Cat

35. Blacktip Reef Shark

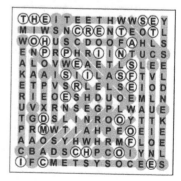

36. Blacktip Reef Shark (continued)

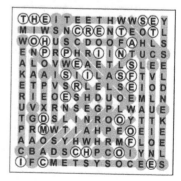

37. Orangutan

38. Orangutan (continued)

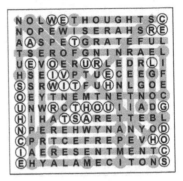

39. Samson the Donkey

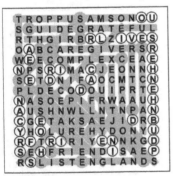

40. Sea Otter

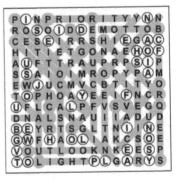

41. Katrina the Cat

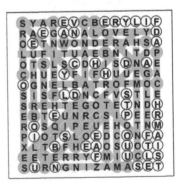

42. Terry the Dog

43. Patches the Dog

44. Johnny the Dog of Many Lives

45. Snuffi the Rabbit

46. Jack the Dog

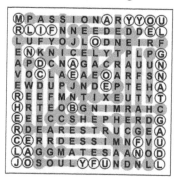

47. Reinie the Cat

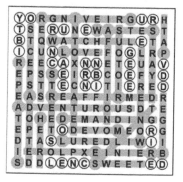

48. Iwao the Dog

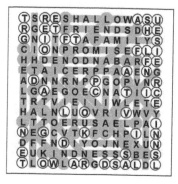

49. Kobi the Dog

50. Roo the Dog

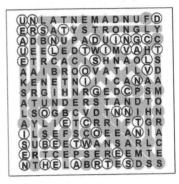

51. Elephant

52. Japanese Giant Salamander

53. American Black Bear

54. Chimpanzee

55. Chimpanzee (continued)

56. Ivan the Raven

57. Kadijah the Cat

58. Great Horned Owl

59. Wild Horse

60. Sugar the Dog

Gratitude and Appreciation

This book reflects the creation of unity through species diversity. Thirty three species in addition to humans contributed to this book.

Our brilliant Puzzle Master is Rick Smith. He carefully crafted each supremely soul-satisfying puzzle. Loved that sacred geometry nine-pointed star puzzle logo? Also created by Rick. Additionally, he designed the book and made the whole brain illustration in *How to Play.*

Our extraordinary co-author Lauren teaches animal communication planet wide and has published several books. All puzzle text animal messages are ©Lauren McCall 2016–2019. They are used by permission. You may contact Lauren at www.IntegratedAnimal.com

Heartfelt thanks to Debra Englander, Consulting Editor, and the fabulous team at Post Hill Press. Your collaborative, entrepreneurial spirit and expert support make you all an author could hope for in a publisher and more.

Vast waves of appreciation for her exquisitely extraordinary editorial contributions flow abundantly to Melissa Morgan. From the elimination of all extraneous words to creating the semi colon bump, she is a precious treasure in my writing process in addition to my life! You may contact her at www.HealingRocks.info or www.MMMHarp.com

Unless otherwise cited, all quotes attributed are in the public domain. Unattributed quotes and illustrations are © 2016–2019 Cristina Smith.

The Yoga of Now – Eckhart Tolle quote from the book *The Power of Now.* Copyright © 2004 by Eckhart Tolle. Reprinted with permission of New World Library, Novato, CA. www.newworldlibrary.com. Used by permission.

These images were created by many talented artists globally and licensed on Dreamstime.com. Model releases are included in Dreamstime license.

Praise – Photo 111807127 © Joruba; Photo 56215161 © Adogslifephoto
Foreword – Photo 52516718 © Benjawan Sittidech
Let's Play – Photo 22024265 © Cathy Keifer
How to Play – Photo 19571679 © Isselee; Photo 15229056 © Isselee; Photo 54272579 © Anankkml
The Power of Animal Wisdom – Photo 84143829 © Rgbe; Photo 52647878 © Barbara Helgason
Can We Really Talk to the Animals? – Photo 40499745 © Karelnoppe; Photo 3133709 © Wong Chee Yen
The Puzzle of Intelligence – Illustration 47893488 © Alain Lacroix; Illustration 116989472 © Martinus Sumbaji; Photo 31190086 © Nichamon Urathamakul
Going Beyond the Beyond – Photo 61046364 © Adogslifephoto; Photo 111576158 © Vasyl Helevachuk; Photo ID 80122725 © Mikumistock; Photo 8766327 © Janet Hastings
The Yoga of Now – Photo 101465009 © Photobeps; Photo 27459087 © A2bb5s; Photo 61378546 © Ammit
End Game – Photo 38796273 © Zcello; Photo 17278416 © Planctonvideo; Photo 2242692 © Vadim Rybakov
Biographies – Photo 73546953 © Zandyz

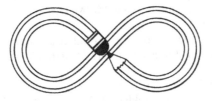

We are deeply grateful to our significant others Bill Jurel, Erika Gilmore, and Helen Dunford for giving us a loving foundation of nourishing support. We appreciate you!

Biographies

Lauren McCall

Lauren exercises her love of puzzles primarily through her work. Though she enjoys a good jigsaw puzzle on rainy winter days and Sudoku on long airplane flights, she spends most of her working life helping people and animals be less of a puzzle to each other. Through workshops, books, and lectures, Lauren travels the world putting the interlocking pieces of interspecies understanding together so that relationships can thrive.

Lauren has loved animals since she was a child in Spain when she briefly cared for a lion cub. Having lived in eight different countries during her life, she has discovered that the desire to understand and experience different cultures is core to her being. That includes the cultures of all species of animals. It is Lauren's belief that the differences between cultures and species are best bridged through various forms of open-minded, and open-hearted, verbal and non-verbal communication. She has discovered that the seemingly puzzling differences between our cultures and species tend to fade away when the common language of love and compassion is used.

Lauren has helped thousands of people connect directly with their beloved animal companions. Heartfelt messages have been shared, bringing about better understanding and communication on all sides. Lauren travels the world teaching her communication techniques, and opening the gate for clearer communication not only between species, but within ourselves.

Melissa Morgan—Editor Extraordinaire

Growing up, my grandfather, who we called Papa Judge, always had time for a game of dominos or several. We got to know and love each other through those drawn-out games. I went on to love Yahtzee and Boggle, spending many a hilarious evening with friends, dictionary in hand. It was always fascinating to see who ended up with which Boggle words!

I hadn't ever done a Sudoku until editing *The Tao of Sudoku*; now I am a convert! I find them to be surprisingly relaxing after a long day. My main puzzling love remains music; I am quite fond of the inside outwards forwards back approach to harmony. I've even been known to take a paintbrush to a music score to communicate the sense of what I hear.

Cristina and Rick Smith

We spent our formative years playing games for hours upon hours together. Card games, jigsaw puzzles, and board games were our favorites. Our parents encouraged us to be curious, creative, and communicative. They gave us the tools, like lots of trips to the library, to nurture our intellects and discover answers for ourselves. They encouraged us to be independent thinkers. Most of all, they gave us the philosophical foundation that we could do anything we wanted.

At first glance, our shared underlying basis isn't easy to see as we are quite different personalities. We have embodied those principles in diverse seeming ways, yet we could be seen as two sides of a coin. In this book, Rick is the puzzle master and book designer. Cristina is the word smith and project orchestrator.

Rick has traveled the planet extensively and Cristina has traveled the inner worlds expansively. Rick developed some of the magic of today's technology and Cristina works the magic of subtle energy healing with people. Rick has worked with his community of longtime friends over the years to design and produce challengingly fun games and Cristina engages her community of longtime friends to create extraordinary events.

We have lots of fun when we get together, still doing puzzles and playing games. We are delighted you decided to play with us!

Contact us at www.GetYogafortheBrain.com. We would love to hear from you!

Yoga for the Brain Books
by Cristina and Rick Smith

www.GetYogafortheBrain.com

The Tao of Sudoku: Yoga for the Brain

The Word Search Oracle: Yoga for the Brain with Darity Wesley

The Word Search Sage: Yoga for the Brain with Ingrid Coffin

Thanks for playing!